MW01234955

Snow After Fire

Kandi Maxwell

Legacy Book Press LLC
Camanche, Iowa

ISBN: 979-8-9867874-0-4
Library of Congress Case Number: 1-12113827463

*For my family
with love and gratitude*

Table Of Contents

Acknowledgments

Many exceptional people have come into my life over the years. Without them, this book would never have come about. I want to thank Barbara and Ray March, my writing mentors and dear friends, who started me on this journey. They have supported me from the beginning with my first stumbling words on the page and have continued to nurture my writing and personal life with patience, knowledge, and kindness. Through Barbara and Rays' Surprise Valley Writer's Conference, I have met many wonderful writers and friends. I want to thank Stephany Wilkes, Patricia Heinicke, Eve Quesnel, Karen Terry, and Vivian Olds—my supporters and the backbone of any confidence I have in my personal writing process. I also want to thank author and best-ever conference faculty, Ana Maria Spagna, who provided me with craft tools and knowledge. She was always available with her warm-hearted spirit and strong encouragement.

I would like to thank my women's writing group in Chico, CA who had to read and critique the words in these pages over a three-year period. Thanks to Susan St. Germaine, the late Cathy Chase, Elisabeth Stewart, Martha Roggli, Mary Jensen, Gwen Willadsen, and Kari Mais. Your encouragement and personal experiences involving the Paradise Camp Fire gave me a deeper understanding of the trauma for those living in, and close to the fire.

I want to thank my strong, lovey, and sometimes crazy family—my daughter, sons, and granddaughters. You are my joy and inspiration. And to Lloyd—my rock and patient partner. Thanks for traveling with me through a life lived with nature—you made our dreams come true.

The following stories were previously published:

"Embers" appeared in *Hippocampus Magazine* 2019
"Snow After Fire" pages 1-18 appeared in *Wordrunner eCha-pbooks* 2020
"After the Swim" appeared in *Raven's Perch* 2020

Note: All rights and ownership have been reverted to me, the author.

Prologue

Fast

I wasn't always tired or ill. For sixty years, I led a furious, fast-paced life and knew, with certainty, that there was something wrong with other people. Why did they move so damned slow? What I hated most were the high school hallways where I had taught English classes. Anytime students spilled into the halls, there were traffic jams. Some students shuffled sluggishly, tucked into their sweatshirt hoods, while others stopped smack in the center of the hall to chat with friends, completely oblivious to others (me) who tried to pass them. And this was a school with a population of two hundred. Light traffic compared to city schools.

I was often shocked at how little work others completed in a day. Work ten hours? No problem for me. Stop for groceries after work, go to a two-hour practice with my women's drum group, walk the dogs, cook dinner, clean up, grade essays. I'd cram it all in. And if someone in my family needed help, I'd up my frantic spin to meet their needs.

Until I couldn't.

After six months in bed and a long hiatus from work, I was diagnosed with Epstein Barr, and worse, I had lost my vibrant mania, lost the lightning-fast creature whom friends had nicknamed Taz, a reference to the Tasmanian Devil in the Looney Tunes cartoons. Although thoughts and images still flashed in swift succession in my mind and I retained my rapid speech, my tornado powers had vanished. Occasionally, I could muster up a small dust devil and hold

1

onto the illusion: mental toughness, perseverance, and fierce loyalty were my superpowers.

Chapter One
Fall 2018

Life in the Maybe

One day, new symptoms emerged: left-side abdominal pain, low blood sugar, spurts of high blood pressure, dizziness. My husband, Lloyd, drove me to the nearest hospital, a forty-five-minute ride down long, winding roads. We made it to the emergency room, where I was admitted to the hospital for an overnight stay for CT scans and lab work. For Lloyd and me, the drive to the emergency room was déjà vu. We had made the same trip a year earlier when I showed similar symptoms. That visit resulted in a four-day hospital stay due to a mini-stroke. The memory heightened my anxiety. Lloyd tried to reassure me with words. "Take a deep breath. We're almost there," he said. He focused on the drive, but there was tension in his body and voice. The test results came back as a host of *maybes*. Once I was released from the hospital, my doctor, Tammy, ordered more tests. As I waited for the results, I tried to create some type of routine, but I had lost my drive. Brain fog kept me from writing; fatigue kept me hidden in the house. Pain, like liquid fire, burned through my muscles and joints and confined me to bed.

When my test results finally arrived, I went to see Tammy. She walked into the room dressed as a fairy. A fluttery, lime-green tutu flared over dark-green tights. Sparkling whimsical wings were attached to her back. A Robin Hood woodsman's cap made her look taller than her six-foot frame. Her festive Halloween outfit conflicted with her businesslike manner. After three months, three CT scans, and an MRI, the results were hardly encouraging.

"You have an adrenal tumor with mottled enhancement. The findings aren't typical of a benign tumor, and this is worrisome for possible malignancy. Don't get worried by the maybes or all the dire information on the Internet," Tammy advised. "We'll order a biopsy to determine definite results."

But I'd already pored over the dire information on websites for words like *adrenal tumor*, *malignancy*, and *cancer.* Something in the grim possibilities pacified me. Anything was better than the unknown.

Hope from the 1960*s*

My *maybe* diagnosis was hard on my adult children. My sons, Jess and Jake, called more frequently, but both had difficulty articulating emotion. My daughter Karen's fears were more evident. I could hear the worry in her silent response to my updates on the possible cancer. We needed a distraction, and Karen had the perfect antidote—tickets to see Joan Baez in a small theater at Chico State University. Joan's ballads of peaceful activism, social justice, and hope offered much-needed light. The concert was scheduled for November 2nd. That afternoon, I drove north to Chico for the concert and an overnight stay with Karen. I had dressed up: flowered bell-bottoms, brown shirt, sandals, and my signature makeup-free face and long frizzy hair. Karen was in sweats when I arrived, but in ten minutes, she looked tastefully sassy in her brightly colored Frida Kahlo T-shirt, an olive-green corduroy jacket, and jeans. Karen looked great in anything.

The night was warm. Star-shaped lights were strung across the brick patio in front of the auditorium. In no time, we were following an usher to our seats, just six rows from the stage. Joan came out with her acoustic guitar, dressed in jeans, boots, and a dark shirt. Her gray hair was cut short. At seventy-seven, she was still hippie cool.

Joan sang songs I used to play and sing for my children: "Baby Blue," "Forever Young," "Blowin' in the Wind," "Diamonds and Rust." As Joan sang, Karen rested her head on my shoulder, held my hand. After the concert, she told me how she had felt like a child again. Joan's clear, strong voice had transported Karen and me to another time where youth, love, and song could change the world. We were ecstatic. Optimistic.

Critical Fire Weather

After the concert, I drove home to our mountain cabin in the Sierra Foothills to wait for the biopsy. We also waited for rain, but the sun blazed hot in a crisp, blue sky. Dry pine needles littered the ground. Not a drop of rain since spring. Spot fires had hopped around our mountain cabin all summer. A few months earlier, our neighbor's house had burned down. The memory of shooting flames and intense heat set me on edge. The occasional sound of planes or helicopters overhead brought teeth-grinding, heart-pumping panic. Lloyd raked leaves, cleaned the gutters, the roof.

The Pacific, Gas & Electric company (PG&E) sent out calls. Critical fire weather. Our power could be turned off in the coming days due to dry conditions and strong winds. That evening, Lloyd readied the camper in case we needed the propane-fueled stove and refrigerator. I set out battery lamps. We were prepared, but the power shutoff was never activated.

Evacuation

November 8, 2018. I was awakened by ringing. I stumbled to the living room, picked up the phone.

"I just want you to know we're okay. We're on our way to Chico." Jess was on the line, and "we" most likely included Jake.

"What do you mean?" I said, blurry-brained and confused. Jess told me there was a fire in Paradise; they were told to evacuate.

"I'll call you when we get to Chico," he said.

Jess hung up, and I set down the phone, dazed. I fumbled around the room, searched for my iPad, found it, and then checked the local news. At first, it seemed routine: "8:04 am. EVACUATION ORDER: Due to a fire in the area, an evacuation order has been issued for all of Pentz Road in Paradise East to Highway 70." My sons lived on a small dead-end road off Pentz.

I read how the one-thousand-acre fire had exploded to five thousand acres. An hour had passed. Chico was a quick twenty-minute drive from Paradise. I sat on the couch in my tattered flannels, stunned and shaken. My ponytail was a mess of tangle. I was a fidgety, fist-clenching basket case. I jumped when Jake called from Barnes and Noble.

"We made it to Chico," he said. Jake told me his ex, Heidi, and my granddaughters, who also lived in Paradise, were on their way to Chico, too.

"The fire is moving fast," I said. "You'd better get a motel room as soon as possible."

Now I was frantic. My hands gripped the iPad as I read with horror the news of the growing mass of flames. By 10:00 a.m., travel out of Paradise had become dangerous. Heavy smoke and fire chased vehicles as the entire community fled. The news became more heart-wrenching by the hour: people were trapped in vehicles; others ran on foot clutching animals and babies. My granddaughters, ages five and eight, were on that road.

Later, Heidi told me, "Heat melted the plastic parts on my car. The fire engulfed both sides of the road, and the air inside the car was suffocating." They made it out, but fears trailed like smoke.

Too Much Missing

It wasn't long before we found out the inevitable. Jess and Jake had lost their home, so they came to stay with my husband and me. My granddaughters, Annie and Marie, and their mother had lost their home as well. Since there was no longer a school, my granddaughters stayed with us a few days a week to relieve the stress of living in motels.

Eight-year-old Annie ran through our combo living room-dining room. Our black-and-white pit bull mutt, Jackson, scratched her leg as she flew by. She burst into tears. I held her in my arms. We sat on the couch together as she gulped in sobs. The scratch was tiny, barely visible, but it was the excuse Annie needed to release the sadness of her loss.

"I miss my pony collection," she said, referring to her My Little Pony toys. "I miss Rainbow Dash and Twilight Sparkle." Her favorites.

"We'll get new ones," I said. Useless words. Too much loss: her tiny grocery store toy collection of Shopkins, her Monster High dolls, her cherished blanket.

I held Annie, let her cry till she slipped into sleep.

Letting Go

Karen, too, had to adjust because of the fire. She was a teacher in Oroville, in the same district as Paradise. School was canceled the day of the fire. She left work and traveled toward Chico, usually a thirty-minute drive. Black smoke had settled into the valley, making even the daytime dark. As the flames blasted west toward the highway, a long detour and traffic extended Karen's commute to a grueling three-and-a-half-hour ride. When she pulled into her driveway, her father, my ex-husband, Craig, sat waiting on a bench on her front porch. He wore his Army Special Forces cap, a T-shirt, and faded jeans. Next to him were his two dogs, a white Chihuahua and a new Lab puppy. These would be the only possessions he saved from the fire. He had nowhere else to go, so Karen welcomed him into her home.

The summer before the fire, Karen had learned she could not have children. There was now emptiness instead of babies. Mothering was Karen's MO. She had worked with children since she was a young teen as a volunteer for The Boys and Girls Club. She worked as a teaching assistant in college and had been a teacher for over a decade.

One day, Karen and I were on a walk. We stopped on a hilltop, watched as the sun fell between the trees below.

"I have to let this go," Karen told me. *This* was two years of trying to get pregnant. "The monthly disappointment is too much."

I wrapped my arms around Karen as her shoulders shook with sadness. I had no words of comfort. For months, Karen had been working through the stages of grief, but the fire had hindered her progress.

She put her focus on her dad. Craig didn't make much money on social security, so Karen paid to get his car fixed. Later, she took him to the Veteran's Center to sign up for services. When FEMA arrived, she was the first to sign up via email. She drove her father to look for places to stay — motel rooms, old migrant-worker barracks, and trailer parks. For the first two weeks after the fire, Karen gave her dad all the energy she could muster. Like the rest of us, she was exhausted.

Some days later, Karen told me over the phone, "I have to go back to work, and I need some time to take care of myself before I return." She felt guilty, like she was abandoning her dad during his loss and grief. Who would protect him? Karen told me she had talked to a counselor, and with help, she was able to confront her dad. "I told him he could do this on his own."

Karen didn't really leave Craig alone. With monetary help from her aunts, Craig's sisters, Karen bought Craig a trailer and helped him move in. It wasn't much, but it was a start.

Welcome Distractions

My home filled with family. They were a welcome distraction from my *maybe cancer.* I could focus on the tangible. We drove to the Disaster Center in Chico. The center was inside an old Sears building, recently cleaned, and the scent of antiseptic lingered. Tall ceilings and vast floors made talking difficult; voices echoed from every direction. Services were set up at long tables. One side of the building was for FEMA: staff stood ready to help individuals sign up for housing or reimbursement for contents lost in their homes. Another side of the building had tables for postal services, the DMV, unemployment assistance. People gathered around large boxes of donations placed throughout the store: blankets, sheets, coats, shoes, and pantry foods were handed out freely. Addresses and DMV records were changed. We collected donations of toothbrushes, razors, socks, and soaps.

Later, there was shopping to be done. An activity I typically found grueling now got me out of bed. There were clothes to buy. Plastic tubs for storage. Toys for the girls. Shopping was my new one-day-a-week profession, something I could commit to even in my weakened state. I still believed the false narrative: somehow, I could smooth the road ahead.

Paradise Lost

December 11. One month after the Camp Fire. I drove to Paradise with Jess. The ride up the ridge was bittersweet. The valley fog opened to blue skies and expansive landscapes. The morning sun gave the hillsides a soft orange glow, and the world looked spring-clean as bright green grasses rose out of the blackened soil. Shades of brown, rust, and tan covered the land. The scorched earth produced a pleasant aroma: a sweet, after-the-rain-campfire scent.

As we ascended, the scenery changed. Utility workers cleared fallen trees and charred brush. Burnt-out cars littered the roadside. Houses had vanished. In their place were thick layers of ash, melted glass, twisted wire, a chimney. We turned onto the street where the boys' house once stood but were disoriented. We had to get out of the car to hunt for the stone driveway. The two-story, A-frame house had shifted into a stretch of ghostly-gray soot. The patch of powdered remains looked small surrounded by the wide-open space. I felt sadness for the loss, but the destruction of irreplaceable items was harder to grasp. Jess and Jake were artists. Their paintings, drawings, and sculptures were gone.

"Maybe we'll find something if we dig up the soot," I said.

Jess and I shoveled through the ash, found bits of pottery, but when cradled in our hands, the clay crumbled to dust.

"Look what I found," Jess said, holding up a small wire dragonfly. His only treasure.

Later, I looked at photos of that day. Jess stands, gazing at the rubble. He wears a green sweatshirt; a gray beanie covers his short brown hair. His shoulders slump. He's holding the cardboard box we had hoped to fill with items spared in the fire. The box is empty.

Anxiety pressed on my chest. I put the photos away, pushed my thumbs into my temples, hoping to relieve the throbbing in my head. I wondered how much more I could endure.

Wiped-out Warrior

The long days were taking their toll; my energy waned. I started spending more mornings in bed. I didn't have the stamina to make coffee, and if I got up, I would have to put the kettle on. Then, I would have to feed the dog, or make the bed. Instead, I fluffed my pillows, picked up my iPad from the bedside, and read or wrote. Lloyd fed the dog and stoked the stove, and the world didn't fall apart.

Before my illness, I was the tenacious warrior, capable and strong, determined to sacrifice self to save others. What a stupid delusion. I decided to desert my post.

Chapter Two
Winter 2018

The Biopsy—January

Lloyd and I left in a dark-morning fog and rain, headed towards Roseville, a two-hour drive. The ride was peaceful until we hit the valley. Once we arrived in city territory, I did my usual raving lunatic routine: pressing my foot on an invisible brake and providing Lloyd with a barrage of unwanted advice—*watch out, slow down, you' re going too fast, stop!* Lloyd sat quietly. That does not mean he was calm. I imagined smoke billowing out of his ears.

Lloyd and I lived in a land of no cell service, so instead of a GPS, I scoured maps. I had written explicit directions on a notecard. I even noted landmarks, but as soon as we left the highway, we were lost. Large buildings and traffic obscured street signs. One-way streets caused confusion. Our frustrations surged, but we eventually found the facility.

From there, things went smoothly. I began the intake process by answering about one million questions, dressing in a size XXXX paper gown and a hairnet. A nurse hooked me up to an IV, and my body calmed. After I was settled and wheeled into surgery, Lloyd left to search for the cafeteria and a much-needed breakfast.

It wasn't long before the surgeon inserted needles into five spots on the tumor. In less than ten minutes, the procedure was completed. I was sent to the "spa" to recover, a small room with a bed surrounded by a light-blue curtain. After an hour's wait, Lloyd and I were sent off with well-wishes.

We drove back through the traffic mess, got turned around again, but eventually found Highway 65, our ticket home.

"This environment is horrible. It's so loud; too many cars and shops. How can people live in this chaos?" I said to Lloyd.

He suggested I quiet down and go to sleep, which I eventually did thanks to the lingering effects of the anesthesia.

What's Wrong with Me?

I was at the local clinic, where I had an appointment for a consultation with Tammy to review the biopsy results. I had checked in and settled into the patient room when a nurse asked, "Were you expecting to get your results back today?"

When I told her I was, she said, "I'm sorry, but our computers have been down all day. Do you want to reschedule?"

Hell no. It's Friday. I won't get the biopsy results until next week. I had no wait-time left in me. I tried to sound polite, controlled.

"I would still like to talk with Tammy."

As I waited in the office, time ticked by. It was 4:45 p.m. *Shit. Tammy will have to call the Roseville Clinic.* I knew the clinic closed at 5:00 p.m. My head pounded. I slumped over my legs, rested my head in my hands.

Tammy came in five minutes later. "Did you see the results on your online health program?" she asked.

"Nothing's been posted yet," I said.

"I've been looking for the results all week," Tammy said. "I'll call Roseville and see if we can get the latest news."

She walked out and left me alone, cringing in my chair. I could hear her voice in the other room, but no distinct words. Finally, Tammy returned, all smiles.

"No cancer," she announced gleefully. "They biopsied five spots on the tumor. All were negative."

"That's great news," I said. "Such a relief."

It was a lie. For four months, I had prepared for cancer, was ready for the sad news, and now, my not-cancer diagnosis left me in despair. *What's wrong with me?*

"Because the tumor is three point six centimeters, Dr. Kim will wait on surgery. We'll get another CT in three months to see if the tumor has grown," Tammy said.

She made an appointment with an endocrinologist to determine why my adrenaline levels were abnormally low. Another appointment with a rheumatologist simmered on the back burner. I wanted it to be over, wanted something definitive.

I wanted a fucking diagnosis.

Slidin' Away

I was in the freezer section of the grocery store. A foreign territory. Large glass cases held rows and rows of foods. There were frozen meals, frozen fruits and vegetables, meats, baked goods, and even Paleo and organic selections. My former self would have been appalled.

In winter, I loved shopping in the produce section of a natural foods store, choosing only the freshest organic vegetables. In summer, Lloyd, a garden enthusiast, worked tirelessly, tending vegetable beds and saving heirloom seeds for the following year's planting. I was the primary harvester, the one who put up food for winter; dried fruits and fruit leathers, frozen and canned vegetables filled our kitchen. Lloyd had built an outdoor, wood-fired oven for baking breads and pizzas. I baked round loaves of artisan bread, made pizzas with garden tomatoes and fresh basil.

Now, standing in the grocery store, I felt my organic hippie self slip off my skin. I searched the frozen food section carefully, reading the ingredients on each package. I chose an organic lasagna, a bag of mixed veggies, tamales. Seeing that these were not the standard TV dinners of my youth gave me a bit of relief.

The following week, I bought my first microwave. I feared radiation would zap nutrition from foods, create carcinogens. *This is for the boys. They can take it with them when they find housing.* I told myself this to relieve the guilt of the purchase.

I struggled to hold onto the person I believed myself to be. Lloyd and I shared a passion for living simply. We were back-to-the-landers, had lived off-grid. Raised cattle, goats, chickens, horses. We were used to hard, physical work: stacking hay, splitting and stacking wood, chopping ice in water troughs on freezing mornings, trudging through snow, digging hard ground. My illness and my family's dislocation from the fire forced changes in both of us.

New Normal

A cold February morning. The ground wet from atmospheric river rains. The sun shone brightly; the world washed clean. I had an appointment with Tammy for my *whatever* diagnosis.

I sat in the small waiting room at the medical clinic. Photos of three young hippie men hung on the wall. One man had shoulder-length brown hair, a bushy David Crosby mustache. The other two men were wavy-haired, tall, and lean. They wore cowboy hats, faded jeans, and fringed leather jackets. These were the original clinic doctors, now in their seventies. After a brief wait, the nurse called my name and led me into another room where Tammy waited.

Tammy and I reviewed my symptoms. The tumor on my left adrenal gland remained, producing an annoying pain, like I had swallowed a crumpled ball of tinfoil. My adrenal hormones were abnormally low. I was worn out, weary, drained, and drowsy.

"You're going to have to create a new normal," Tammy said. "Plan on adding activities back into your life slowly over the next six months. You will feel better if you can get out more."

I told Tammy about the sharp pains beneath my ribs, my inflamed joints, and the ache deep inside my bones. How it took an enormous effort to get out of bed.

"Is your family still with you?" she asked.

"My sons are living with us. My granddaughters have moved for the fifth time. They're in a motel right now, so they come here often."

With thirty thousand people dislocated from the fire, finding homes seemed impossible, and FEMA trailers wouldn't be available for months. We were at a breaking point. The day before my appointment, Heidi, my granddaughters' mother, told me, "I just want one good night's sleep. I don't know how long I can keep this up."

"That must be stressful," Tammy said. "I'm sure that has an influence on your energy level."

Tammy was right. I needed to accomplish at least one thing each day. To come to terms with my limitations and with life in this in-between place where pushing forward was excruciatingly slow.

Dreams

In daydreams, I had planned to backpack the Pacific Crest Trail after retirement. That was out, so I looked for what was in. More reading, writing, and, of course, more family time. And there was sitting in the sun with Lloyd on cool winter days. Because we live in forestland, we moved our chairs around the yard, followed the sun's warmth. I sipped coffee while Lloyd smoked his herb, and the sunlight did its healing magic. We talked about moving higher up the mountain, getting more land, living off-grid again.

Was this delusional thinking? I shared my thoughts in an email with a dear friend who lived in the high country.

"No one ever said there were limit lines to dreams," he wrote. His words sank in, and my lips involuntarily turned up, and I felt something like hope.

It was four months since the fire, seven months since my visit to the ER; not much had changed. Except the snow was falling. Tiny cotton bits lightly dropped onto the ground. I couldn't stop watching it, the way it descended so light and sleepy, how it quieted the house and my mind, how it made the world look unblemished and new.

Chapter Three
Spring 2019

Embers

March 2019. A fine mist and a hint of sun. After several days of heavy rain, the early spring day began to clear. My granddaughters were with us. Jake had decided to take his daughters to the community park. I helped five-year-old Marie pull up her fleece leggings and zipped her into a dark-blue sweatshirt, the one with the large, round sequins. Marie hated shoes, but I eventually slipped on her silver tennies with the promise of ice cream. We walked to the car, our feet sinking deep into soggy pine needles.

As I set Marie in her car seat, she said, "Pony," with a wistful, drawn-out sigh. Suddenly, her voice rose, and she cried, "Pony, pony, pony!" Marie pointed under the driver's seat. I looked where she pointed but saw only a tiny plastic paddle.

"I'll get it," I said.

I reached under the seat for the paddle and handed it to Marie. Her eyes brimmed with tears. She grasped the paddle tightly, folded herself in, and rocked back and forth. Marie is autistic and speaks in short phrases.

"Pony gone," she said.

"Yes, pony is gone."

She looked at me for reassurance. "Fire gone?" she asked.

"Yes, fire is gone."

When the Camp Fire forced Jake and his entire family, including my sweet Marie, to evacuate, there wasn't time to think about what to take or what to leave behind. Marie and Annie grabbed a few toys and were quickly loaded into the family car. Strong winds made the fire erratic, and a few neighboring homes were already engulfed in flames.

Her family got stuck in the gridlock as the entire town tried to flee the inferno. Marie and Annie, draped in sopping-wet blankets to block the heat, were steamed by the suffocating swelter. Smoke and sparks whirled around them as their car crawled through the conflagration. They zigzagged around burnt-out cars blocking the road. Those who had abandoned their vehicles ran on foot, some with babies in their arms. The typical thirty-minute drive to Chico, where they were headed, took over three hours. When I imagined my family in this scene, my heart was pierced with pain.

Marie had lost her belongings, her home, the park we played in, the school she attended. But Marie's memories were in the moment.

"Fire gone?" she repeated.

I closed my eyes, pressed my fingers into the ache under my ribs. We'd had this conversation before, and the bites stung each time. I hugged Marie gently. When I spoke, my words were worn and weak.

"Yes, the fire is gone."

In Paradise, Marie had attended a school for autistic children, where she thrived. Now, without a home or her school routine, she was regressing. She was wearing diapers again, she wanted her bottle, and she rarely slept.

A sudden sadness overwhelmed me.

I was exhausted by so much *gone*.

It would be days before I could connect the paddle to the pony and to my granddaughter's grief. Annie would tell me later about Pinkie Pie Pony and the Row and Ride Swan Boat.

"The boat played music when she pushed it, and Pinkie Pie Pony rowed the boat."

I could see the before: Marie pushing her little boat around the large living room floor of her family home. And the after: five moves to five different places since her home was leveled to ash.

The fire was gone, but the embers still flared.

After the Swim

Late May 2019. Cumulus clouds drifted past a pale sun. It was a chilly day for swimming, but I couldn't resist traveling to the lake for a good soaking. I yearned for the solace I'd find there. I invited Annie to join me. She needed the large expanse of water, and time to stretch her limbs and move freely.

In the six months since the deadly blaze, her family had moved from a one-bedroom apartment with other family members to three different motels. After that, her household of five settled into an RV on a lot at her stepfather's work. Annie was weary of cramped trailer living. As a hyperactive child, she craved a place to skip and scurry. Our cabin was small, but there was a half-acre yard, perfect for running through the sprinklers or playing tag. On this day, Annie needed to expend more energy than usual.

Her lips quivered. "I hate being indoors and sitting on my bed all day. I'd rather go to school and do math than spend one more minute in the trailer," she said.

At school, there was recess. At home, play outdoors was restricted due to buses and cars on the lot where their RV was parked.

"Summer's coming soon," I said, "then you can visit more often." We lived an hour away from Chico, where Annie's family was temporarily sheltered.

I tossed towels, swim-noodles, camp chairs, and a cooler filled with blueberries, croissants, and juice into the back of my Jeep. As we bounced down the cracked and crumbled road headed toward the lake, occasional bursts of sunlight popped through the clouds. Lake Francis lies at the border of Tahoe National Forest. Tall pines, willows, and thick stands of cattails surround the shoreline. Annie and I found a perfect spot: a flat space under the pines with a grassy, green bank. Already in our swimsuits, we strolled to the water and waded in. We wobbled over sharp stones in our winter-softened feet, but once past the rock, the lake bottom turned to slime.

"It feels like I'm walking on bird poop," Annie said.

"It's gooey, red clay," I said, as my feet sank into sticky softness.

Holding our noodles, Annie and I moved easily through the warm shallows, but when we stepped deeper, where water hit our hips, cold flooded out the warmth.

"We'll have to dunk in," I said.

Annie, always ready to please, held my hand. We counted, "One, two, three," and plunged into the icy lake. Annie popped up like a Jack-in-the-box; her teeth chattered, and goose bumps covered her arms.

After a year without swimming, Annie was fearful, so we practiced paddling and kicking in the shoal where she could touch the bottom.

"You're doing great, "I said. "You're swimming. Just hold your noodle underneath your arms for support."

"I'm swimming. I'm swimming," Annie said, as her lips curved into a joyful smile.

As her confidence grew, we swam in deeper waters. The clouds overhead parted and lit the waves with golden ribbons. Our arms moved like butterflies' wings; our legs kicked like frogs' legs. I showed Annie how to float on her back, head facing the sun, eyes closed, arms extended. We were free and buoyant, and for a while, silent, as the tranquil sensation of the water's ripples rocked us gently toward the reeds. And eventually, into a small flock of geese who flapped their wings and honked, breaking our calm.

For over an hour, we swam with the geese, drifted with the current, and splashed in the shallows. As clouds covered the sun, the water turned cold, but we hesitated to leave. After a while, Annie began to shake and shiver. Her lips were blue; I suggested it was time to go. I wrapped her in towels and a fleece blanket, placed a woolen cap on her head. She slipped on her flip-flops and walked toward the Jeep. I pulled down the tailgate and helped her into the back, then turned on the engine and heater. Annie tugged off her wet swimsuit, and I draped her in a sweater. The windows steamed as Annie ate croissants, and blueberries stained her fingers dark purple. We soaked up the warmth inside the Jeep until our goose bumps faded.

Later, as we drove home in the toasty car, I imagined other adventures for Annie: kayaking on the lake, hiking the path along the Yuba River, lying on sun-warmed granite boulders in the river's emerald pools.

I knew that Annie's home life would be difficult for some time, as housing was impossible to find. The promised FEMA mobile home parks for the Camp Fire survivors were slow in coming. The first small park had opened just weeks earlier. More home parks were planned, but it was hard to find sites to place so many temporary housing units. It would take many more months to find acceptable locations and install the necessary infrastructure, like water, sewer, and electricity.

I'd hoped our forays into nature would give Annie some space to play and release her excess energy, and possibly, a place for grounding in an unpredictable world.

From the backseat, I heard Annie's soft breaths. Looking in the rearview mirror, I noticed her closed eyes as she cuddled in her blanket. Calm and relaxed, I sank into my seat, savoring the landscape that unfurled along the path.

Trauma

Flash forward—three and a half years after the Camp Fire, March 2022. I took Annie and a school friend, Ellie, to a trampoline park. Ellie had only recently returned to Paradise, her family's hometown for generations. As we drove down Skyway towards our destination, Ellie, a tall, large-boned girl with curly red hair, described her experiences escaping the Camp Fire.

"We had to get out of the car because we weren't moving and the fire was behind us," Ellie said in her rambling, fast-talking monologue. "We just started running." Later, I would learn the *we* included her mother and an older brother and sister. Like Annie, Ellie was eight years old at the time. She continued, "We ran down Skyway until we saw someone we knew. She stopped, and we rushed into her car. We made it out."

Ellie told more of her story on our forty-minute drive. As she talked, she pointed out a burnt lot where her grandmother used to attend church, a rebuilt store that "really looks different," and a still-standing funeral home, black smoke burning out of a chimney behind the building where "they cremate people." Her sentences were random, but the story was easy to piece together.

"After the fire, we moved all over. A lot of terrible things happened, but we had an adventure. We even went to Alaska." Ellie was making the best of it, but there was an edge in her voice. "We camped a lot. I liked hanging out by the river." She mentioned her mother's poor choices, physical abuse, and drugs. She was now living with her father, who had also lost his home in the fire, but had recently bought a new home.

Ellie's family's tale of trauma was a familiar one. Many Camp Fire survivors had reported experiencing PTSD, including increased drug and alcohol use, anxiety, depression, anger, and grief. I'd seen those traits in my own family and knew the stories of others who had fled the fire and were still living with their wounds: a sixty-nine-year-old grandmother, forced to live in her car, feared for her safety; two young men who had lost their rental homes turned to drugs for comfort and to emotionally check out. Some families were unable to communicate and turned to verbal abuse. Karen told me about her students who still had difficulty with concentration and who struggled to find stability. Cried.

A study published in February 2021 by the *International Journal of Environmental Research and Public Health* found that a large number of Camp Fire survivors suffered from mental health disorders. "The amount of PTSD we saw in individuals was striking and very significant," said Jyoti Mishra, senior author of the study and a professor in the department of psychiatry at UC San Diego School of Medicine. "It was on par with what we'd expect to see in war veterans, but now we're seeing it in communities where individuals are exposed to wildfires."

The collective grief of an entire community could be overwhelming. Too much need. Not enough therapists, rehab programs, or housing for the homeless. Not everyone made it. I knew a veteran who died of suicide after the fire. As I write, I feel sad. I need to hear more success stories, but they're slow to come.

Marie and the Birds

My blissful sleep was interrupted by the cackle of a loud, old crone. I peeked at the clock: 7:00 a.m. My fogged brain imagined some large, flightless fowl at the window, but I was sleeping upstairs in our cabin, surrounded by thick stands of cedar and pine. The treetops were too high for our clipped-wing hens, who might give a good flap but could barely lift their heavy bodies off the ground.

Across the room from me, Marie slept. Her wrists were crossed, and her fists nestled under her chin. Blonde hair spread in wisps around her face. Her eyes were closed; her soft breaths sounded like kitten purrs.

When awake, Marie was hyperenergetic, in constant motion, spinning, and jumping repeatedly. Sleep was hard to come by. Many nights, she would be wide-awake as she played with her My Little Pony figures past 3:30 a.m. I had hoped she would sleep in late, but no such luck.

Marie heard the strange noise at the window and opened her eyes.

"Did you hear that?" I asked. I didn't expect an answer, as Marie was language delayed. She could, however, speak a few words. "Let's go investigate," I said.

Suddenly, Jackson barked in earnest. Marie popped up and ran down the stairs. I followed behind, stiff and slow. By the time I got to the front door, the lone cackle had increased in intensity, and I realized that the gang of large-bodied, turkey-like birds, the guinea fowl from next door, had invaded our yard.

I opened the door, and Jackson bolted, Marie right behind him. Barefoot and still in pajamas, she ran into the yard as Jackson chased after the large birds. He growled and got close enough to grab one. Marie was standing near Jackson, laughing and clapping her hands. *Shit. My granddaughter will watch Jackson kill this bird. It will crush her heart.*

Jackson lunged at a large, black hen, but guinea fowl are strong fliers, and the bird flew into the trees. He went after another bird; it flew to the roof. Marie was ecstatic. Her hands waved like wings.

"Fly, fly," she said, running toward the birds without fear as the crazy-fast gang ran in retreat. She continued her mantra, "Fly, fly." The birds flew at her command, scattering in the trees and on the rooftop.

The chaos lasted only a few minutes. Soon, the flock of fowl were safe together on the other side of the fence, where they continued to chatter and screech as they waddled away. Later, after the noise quieted, and Marie settled down to watch *SpongeBob* on her small DVD player, I smiled at the image of Marie and the birds. She was fearless and bold; she had chased away the menacing fowl. I could see that part of her now—her strength. She would be okay.

Chapter Four

Summer 2019

Reflections

I looked back through photos: Annie and Marie running through the sprinklers, Annie frosting cookies in our cabin's bright kitchen, Marie racing through the house in her blue Cat Boy costume, complete with mask. Those were happy times.

Other times were hard. Lloyd wasn't in the photos. He needed space that our crowded house couldn't offer. Moving through our tiny house felt suffocating. One morning, he drove his truck to town and returned with a twenty-eight-foot fifth wheel. We had owned a fifth wheel in the past, so he already had a hitch installed in the bed of his truck. Lloyd parked the RV in the driveway and moved in. It was there where he slept, made his morning coffee, and enjoyed the self-time he craved. Lloyd came into the house for meals and showers. Our time together faded. I couldn't reach across the expanding crevasse. I tried to be the perfect wife/parent/grandparent. Tried to juggle the needs of each of my family members. Often, I'd come up short. Emotional stamina was an airy hope. I tried to push past the exhaustion, but there wasn't much forward momentum. I held on by a fine wire, fearing any minute it would break.

Chapter Five
Fall 2019

Seeking Solace

In September of 2019, my sons and grandchildren moved into their long-anticipated FEMA trailers. Our home quieted. However, instead of relief, weariness and depression trapped me inside the house. I forced myself to get out of bed. Then I wondered, why bother?

October. An electric outage was planned by PG&E. High winds and dry brush made our home a fire risk. At 3:00 p.m., a phone recording on our message machine said to be ready for the shut-off sometime in the evening. I rushed to get in three loads of laundry before the outage hit. I hadn't done laundry in days, as Lloyd had discovered our water pipe was plugged by a big, fat toad. He had just finished flushing the pipes. I mopped up the water that had flooded the laundry room floor.

While the dryer whirled, I set camp lamps on counters and tables with extra batteries nearby. I checked the propane tanks in our camper. Full. That meant I could cook meals on the gas stove.

When the electricity snapped off at 5:00 p.m., the quiet came quick. The dryer stopped turning; the refrigerator ceased its hum. I sat on the couch and listened to what some might call *nothing*. I sank into the stillness.

The silence brought memories. Images of towering pines and an off-grid log cabin where Lloyd and I lived in the Tahoe National Forest. We had a propane stove and refrigerator; soft solar light glowed from bulbs that hung from the ceiling; a fire crackled in the large woodstove in the center of the main room, a combination kitchen, living, and dining room. Winter nights often produced several feet of sound-absorbing snow. Thick icicles hung from the roof.

Life could be exhausting back then. I worked full time, and several nights each week, I made the three-hour, round-trip drive to take graduate classes down the mountain. It would be midnight by the time I would park my truck near the main road to hike up the hill to our cabin. More than once, my vehicle spun out on the black, icy roads. Still, this lifestyle was my restoration.

I missed the solitude of our off-grid cabin and longed for the seclusion of backcountry roads. Even though our current home was nestled in thick forest, without streetlights or too-close neighbors, we were on a paved road. Cars and the sound of neighbor's voices made me cranky. When Lloyd and I retired and moved from five thousand feet elevation to twenty-four hundred feet, life was easier. The warmer winters meant less firewood to cut and split. Our four-wheel-drive trucks and snow tires were no longer necessary. We didn't have to drain faucets, disconnect garden hoses, heat-tape water pipes, or break the ice in the horses' troughs. But we were restless, and our thoughts often returned to off-grid living.

Common sense might have told us to enjoy this softer life. After all, we were senior citizens. What if we couldn't keep up with the work off-grid living demanded? What if our health failed? We both had arthritis and had experienced minor strokes. Lloyd had COPD and neuropathy. I had chronic fatigue. And yet...overall, we were healthy. We could walk, bend, and lift small loads.

Was it possible?

If not possible, necessary. We needed *our* lives back. After almost a year of extending so much of ourselves to my family, we were drained. We didn't want to age this way. We wanted to live life on our own terms.

"Live the dream," Lloyd said. So, after four years in our rural-residential cabin, this place we thought we'd live out our remaining years, Lloyd purchased land on a hilltop where the sun set fire-orange over the valley below us. Our first idea was reasonable. We would keep our home on the paved road and camp out on the off-grid property as recreation. The problem was, once we were out on the mountain, nature sucked us in, and we didn't want to leave. We would gladly trade convenience for land and solace.

Hiding

October. I wanted to stay on the land, stay off-grid, but we still had our other home to care for. Plants needed water, chickens needed tending, and laundry needed washing. Lloyd spent most of his time on the property; I joined him a couple days a week. Even though we were only a fifteen-minute drive apart, the barrier between us was grew wider.

Lloyd was hiding in the woods. From me. I didn't blame him. I attempted to run away from myself as well but couldn't pull it off. Panic had become my pattern. Nausea, worry, and stabbing chest pains were relentless. I couldn't catch my breath. Worse was my irritability. Sounds annoyed me: barking dogs, cars in the distance, and the nonstop chattering of the neighbor's guinea hens had me pulling at my hair. I was short-tempered and overwhelmed. Inside, I wanted to be tender and kind, but I didn't have the energy to voice complete sentences. My words came out short and sharp.

Lloyd had a good excuse to be away. He was working on the land. There were dead and dying shrubs to clear, trees to prune, pine needles to rake. A strong, defensible space was needed around the old trailer on the property. It was fall. Pinecones and tree limbs littered the ground. The work had to be done, but mostly, Lloyd needed time alone.

After the Camp Fire, my first reaction was providing immediate shelter to my sons and granddaughters. It was temporary. We could do this. But as the months dragged on without rental options or FEMA housing, Lloyd believed my efforts to help my family were enabling them. He wanted me to develop stronger boundaries. I didn't. Like other families tossed together into cramped spaces, maintaining balance to meet each family member's needs was difficult, but my sons had no other space to go. Lloyd had lost his space—his sense of place in his own home. An emotional wall divided us. We struggled to meet inthe middle.

Lloyd and I tried to rekindle our relationship while out on the property. The mornings began with a dull-gray light that flickered through the tall Madrone and oaks. The smell of strong coffee wafted through the kitchen. After I stirred cashew milk and stevia into each mug, we stepped outdoors and onto the small, covered porch. I rocked in a camp rocker. My tangled, uncombed hair was pulled back in a ponytail; I wore faded jeans and an old sweater. Lloyd reclined in his lawn chair wearing his daily uniform: a plaid flannel shirt and brown Carhartt work jeans. Always tidier than me, Lloyd's hair was tied back in a thin, neat braid.

"I was thinking we should sell the Jeep," Lloyd said. We had a 2016 Jeep Patriot, paid for. It was a four-wheel drive, but a city car, too low for the rocks and ruts that filled our dirt road. "We've got the Tacoma and the Dodge. That's all we really need."

I agreed. We would be back to driving trucks. No need for a town car. It would give us a bit of cash to put into the trailer. We needed a new woodstove, new propane tanks, batteries for the solar.

"I was thinking we should keep the house at least a year or two, see what happens. We can afford both," Lloyd said.

"That might be a good idea," I said. "We need to see this road in winter. Plus, we can do laundry, store belongings like the larger tools at the house. We can take indoor showers, too. We may want that when the rains come."

Lloyd was including me in *his* project. He was the one who had saved the money to buy the land, and it had left me feeling like I was alone, dangling from a kite string. I had held on with a wild swing, without control or input into our future. Now Lloyd was asking for my thoughts and opinions. Maybe the walls were coming down. We would be all right.

We weren't. A few days later, I called Lloyd while he was out at the trailer.

"What are you doing?" I said.

"I'm just sitting here," he said.

He knew we were going to the dump this morning. Did he forget?

"It's Sunday. Last night you said you'd see me tomorrow. Remember, we planned a dump run?"

"I forgot about that. I'll be over in a bit."

Something was off. Lloyd always kept his commitments. When Lloyd arrived, he was clearly agitated. I was worried, but we loaded the trash cans into the back of the truck, then drove toward the waste transfer station.

Lloyd broke the silence. "I can't talk to you. You don't hear what I'm saying," he said. "I tried to write down what I need to say." Lloyd was scrolling through his iPhone, found what he was searching for, handed it to me.

"I don't have my glasses. I'm not sure I can read this."

But I put together enough of his words to understand their meaning. Tears blinded my eyes. I stopped reading. My voice cracked; sobs made speaking impossible. I finally formed a few words.

"You're leaving me?"

"We're separating," Lloyd said. "We need some time apart." As I wept desperately, Lloyd turned the truck around and drove back to the house.

"Take some time. I'll be back soon, and we can talk," he said.

I stumbled out of the truck, shocked, but somehow, deep down, I knew this was coming. Yet I didn't know. Confusion ripped my heart. I hid in the house. As I lay on my bed, I curled into a tight ball, clutching my sweater as if by holding it, I could somehow hold myself together.

Better

Lloyd and I couldn't talk. I was too emotional: fear, panic, and pain pushed me over the edge. Lloyd was too emotionally drained. He felt nothing. So, we made plans to get together the following week.

The day of our planned afternoon visit, my morning was disastrous. I tried to write notes for my counseling appointing the next day, but as I sat at the dining table attempting to arrange my muddled thoughts on paper, my emotions took me on a wild roller-coaster ride. Tears blinded my eyes as I tried to write. I missed my husband. Then, I'd look out the large front window where several old chestnut trees stood. Their broad leaves were still green and formed a protective barrier around me. I had always thought of trees as refuge; I could feel their long limbs hold me. Momentarily, I was calm. Then, the wind stirred, and yellow-brown spiked hulls fell to the ground. I remembered it was autumn and the trees would soon shed their leaves. I worried about winter. How would I manage with only gray, barren branches? For about an hour, I rode these emotional waves. Finally, I pulled myself together, and there was some cohesion on the page and a bit of resolve in my unease.

Lloyd arrived in his Dodge truck, parked, and let Jackson out of the back seat. Jackson seemed happy to be home. He eagerly sniffed the grass in the yard and then rolled in the red dirt. Lloyd greeted me with a kiss; I went into the house to make coffee. Before our separation, our coffee breaks had been an afternoon ritual, a time set aside to relax and chat.

The day was warm, so we sat on the porch. The leaves and thorny nuts on the chestnut trees twirled in the wind. The smell of possible rain was in the air. In this setting, with just the two of us, I felt the safety of the familiar.

I plunged in. "I'm going to my counseling appointment tomorrow," I said. "I need to know what I'll be working through. Please be honest. Am I working on closure or on boundary issues with my family, so you won't feel pushed out of our relationship?"

"Let's start with boundaries," Lloyd said.

It was enough. We changed the subject, talked about Lloyd's work on the property. He had been cleaning out the shed where the solar batteries and their components were kept. The building had been vandalized during its three-year vacancy. Lloyd had to sort through the wreckage to find out what was usable and what he needed to buy.

"It will probably take a while to get the water, propane, and solar set up," Lloyd said. "No hurry. I like the camp-style living. I really enjoy the outdoor shower." Then, he added, "You seem to be doing better."

For now, I thought. My life was a series of undulating hills. My emotions swung between periods of mild depression and hypomania, but there was no consistent pattern. By 2:30 a.m. the next morning, a raw edginess startled me awake. *Better* didn't last long.

A few days later, we had another power shutdown. Almost a year since the Paradise Camp Fire, a few days shy of November, and still no rain. Dry grasses and leaves covered the soil. Swift, dangerous winds roared through the trees. Throughout the night, branches broke and crashed onto the roof. The house whined and creaked. Every so often, I heard a loud thud. I looked out the window to assess the damages, but all I saw was blackness.

Lloyd had gone to Oregon to visit his brother, so Jackson was with me. We huddled in the bedroom, Jackson snug against my side. It was cold, but I didn't start a fire in the woodstove, as dry pine needles and crispy leaves lay scattered on the roof. I knew that a spark could be deadly. So, Jackson and I kept to the back bedroom.

He snored softly as I read in the not-so-bright light of a battery lamp. Eventually, I went to sleep, but woke several times during the night to a clatter or clash.

The wind still wailed in the morning, but the light brought some sense of relief. I climbed out of bed, while Jackson chose to stay snuggled in the soft bedspread. I opened the door to the back porch and put the kettle on my one-burner camp stove. I made coffee, then returned to the bedroom. Sipping the hot drink slowly, I stared out the window, watched the tall cedars bend in the wind. Their soft, ferny fingers moved with stunning flexibility. I wanted to be like the cedar, to flow when gale force winds pushed against me. Instead, I often cracked like the dry limbs of the oak that fell to pieces on the ground.

After some morning reading, I went outdoors and stupidly raked leaves and sticks into a pile. I knew the activity was fruitless; the winds were ferocious, but I needed to move. When finished, I climbed a ladder and swept off the dirt and grit that stuck behind the stove pipe on the roof, but I was still afraid to start a fire.

Back inside the house, I was freezing. Jackson, too. He drove me crazy, crowding next to me on the couch, his heavy head in my lap, my legs asleep.

I thought about *better.* What was better? Freezing in the house due to fear of fire or building a fire in the woodstove? I built the fire. Then, I worried about burning down our little town because if a fire broke out, I couldn't dial 911. The phone was dead, and we did not have cell service in our community. I thought about the new stove, its stovepipe that towered at least six feet above the roof. It should be safe. Then, I remembered my friend in Mount Shasta whose hand-built cabin burned to ashes after a fire started in his woodstove.

I wondered if there was any such thing as better.

Was it better to ask my children to leave our home after losing theirs in a fire, to turn them loose during a time of such upheaval? Or was it better to build boundaries so Lloyd and I could have a home, a space for ourselves? Should I take care of my needs for rest and quiet? Or was it better to live in a crowded home in exchange for the peace I felt knowing that my sons and granddaughters had a roof over their heads?

And there was this.

Maybe there is no *better.* All we have are choices that we must live with and then accept the consequences those choices bring. Maybe better is merely acceptance.

Just before sundown, Lloyd returned from Oregon. He picked up Jackson, and they left for the property. As I watched Lloyd drive away, I wondered for the first time if better might be living alone.

Wolf Medicine

I knew Lloyd would stay on the land. I wanted him to have the time to heal, but the word *separation* was hard to absorb. It sounded foreboding—the first stage of failure. I wanted Lloyd to be content, wanted us to age together in hippie bliss, walking naked in the woods in summer, cooking on a woodstove in winter. On dark nights, alone in my bed, I just wanted my wolf dog, Lady. She died a year earlier after a two-year battle with heart failure. She was my healing animal, sweet and good-natured. If I had a bad day, she seemed to sense it; she'd gently lick my hands, give my face a few soft kisses. If I brushed her thick coat or scratched her belly, she was euphoric. I longed for my companion. Lloyd had taken Jackson with him on the land.

How would I make it through the winter without a dog?

Two o'clock in the morning. I was wide awake, looking through the available animals on the Lake Tahoe Wolf Rescue site, but none of the animals seemed to suit my needs. Some were too old or didn't play well with others. Most needed extensive training. I skimmed the Internet, gazing at wolf photos. I clicked on a site about wolf medicine. As I scanned the words, a few phrases struck me. I had heard similar lore before, and in my experience with wolf dogs, the words rang true: wolves remind us that everything in nature has some sense of order, even during chaos. The wolf spirit can teach us how to balance our personal needs with those of family.

The previous year had left me emotionally and physically drained, and my own needs were put on hold. I needed a partner and imagined a sweet pup like Lady lying next to me in bed, her warmth keeping me snug and safe on a cold night. Or maybe, this dog and I would walk along the lake, the shoreline soft and spongy and spattered with duck shit. I would wear faded jeans and an old pair of Teva sandals that would sink into the mud. Still sleepless, I tried to get organized and wrote a list:

- Continue my search for a dog.
- Call my daughter, Karen, for support.
- Call my sons to discuss healthy boundaries. Allow them the opportunity to solve their own issues.
- Call my ex-daughter-in-law. Set limits on her visits to my home.
- Make an appointment with my doctor.
- Get out of the house.

By the end of day two, most of the tasks on my list were completed, but feelings of loss and sadness overwhelmed me. I wept for Lloyd, for Lady, and for a wolf dog I had yet to find.

I needed sleep.

I walked into the bathroom, opened the medicine cabinet, found the oblong blue pills, said, "Fuck it," and downed one with water. For the past year, I had taken Aleve PM for severe back pain. When I learned that it was an anticholinergic, a drug that could increase risk of dementia in older people, I stopped using it. But why not take it? I was already old and crazy.

I slept soundly, waking at 7:30 a.m. the following morning. I was elated. The pure ecstasy of a full night's sleep got me out of bed. I put on a warm fleece robe, made coffee, brought it into the bedroom where I propped up my pillows and read in bed. I faced a window with a view of cedars, oaks, and pines. It was a beautiful morning.

Canine Medicine

I had lived with Lloyd for twenty years, and now, I didn't even have a goddamn dog. As soon as the power turned back on, I would look again at the wolf rescue site. Maybe check other options, too.

I didn't get a wolf dog. I got Poochie. Who calls a dog Poochie? For a two-year-old miniature husky, the name seemed insulting. Poochie needed a bigger name, something more fitting for her breed. A husky is a husky, no matter the size. Many city dwellers get these small dogs, not realizing they have huge needs. Her previous owners weren't abusive, but they were deceived by Poochie's size. She was left in a tiny suburban backyard while her caretakers worked all day. Huskies could be crazy-hyper and destructive if they didn't get outdoors and move. This was a breed I understood.

A week earlier, I had finally admitted to myself that it was unlikely I could train another ninety-pound dog, so I branched out my search beyond wolf dogs. I looked on the Internet for smaller dogs that needed homes. I scrolled through photos, and when I saw Poochie's large brown eyes circled by her striking white mask, I knew she was the one. The owners wanted Poochie placed with someone who could provide room to run. I had a fenced half acre and a large kennel, and she could run on the ten-acre property. We would make a good match.

I picked up Poochie on an early fall morning. I met with her owner, J. T., at a Chevron gas station forty minutes from my home. Poochie sat in the back of a black truck. She wore a red harness that attached to her leash. I came over and scratched behind her ears, cooed to her in my silly baby-dog voice. She loved the attention, and when I walked her over to my Jeep, she jumped right in. After a quick goodbye to J. T., Poochie and I went for a long walk at a nearby park. The air was brisk, and the park's man-made lake shimmered silver in the sun. Afterwards, we made a trip to Petco to buy a new crate, a dog bed, treats, and other necessities.

According to J. T., Poochie was a yard dog. She was only housed in the summer when she stayed in her crate on hot days. Poochie didn't know she wasn't a house dog. When we walked into my home after our long drive, she jumped right onto the couch as nice as could be, and even though I made a cozy bed for her in the crate, she preferred to snuggle next to me in the evening. For the first time since my husband left, I no longer felt alone.

Of course, adopting a two-year-old dog wasn't all bliss. Her preferred way to get my attention was to chew on my clothes and bark. Poochie needed manners, as she hadn't had much socialization. There were times when she was so annoying that I had to put her in the yard for a time-out, but the most effective training was exercise. We walked thirty minutes every morning and another half hour in the afternoon. I taught Poochie to fetch a ball, and she ran around our half-acre yard.

Her best days were out on the land. Lloyd and I had started to spend more time together. On the mountain, Poochie ran. Plus, Jackson made a great playmate. And something else happened. While Lloyd and I walked through the brown, crunchy leaves and watched our dogs run, I felt a slight shift in our relationship. We were in that place we knew well, a place where neighbors were scarce and unseen, a forest place where the trees grew tall and brush was dense, where sunlight fell on the red, dusty earth in glittering rays. In our comfort zone, we became more relaxed and open. Shoulders slipped slightly; an occasional smile shared. Trees, grass, wind. Dogs running free. A fragile hope.

Hope Junkies

A red flag Monday in November. The sun shone bright in a crisp blue sky. Heavy winds and low humidity made for high fire danger. Home alone at the cabin, I worried about a flaming forest, but instead of fire, we were hit by a winter storm. On Tuesday, the electricity was off again, as the trees, laden with snow, had toppled over power lines. I had recently bought food for a Thanksgiving meal. I filled the refrigerator with ice from the freezer, placed the turkey on top, and prayed for electrical power. Then, I thought about fire. And snow.

The contrast seemed an appropriate metaphor for my marriage. A small flame of hope would flicker, only to be quenched by a spit of snow.

Wednesday morning came and still no power, but I had an appointment with Tammy. We did blood work, then talked about my upcoming abdominal CT scan for the one-year follow-up on my benign adrenal tumor. Tammy asked about my emotional state.

"How's things with your husband?"

I fluttered my hand. "It fluctuates."

"What does he want?" she said.

"He says he doesn't want a divorce, but he wants certainty that I won't take my family into our home again. He's waiting for May, to see what will happen when the lease on their FEMA trailers expires. That's six months from now. I need a more tangible way to move forward, some plan for this in-between time."

"Can you spend time with Lloyd without expectations? That way, you'll have more emotional stability. You need to focus on taking care of yourself. Can you do that?"

"Maybe. I need to try something. These difficulties are crushing me," I said.

"We're hope junkies," Tammy said. "We see a bit of light and believe everything will work out. We hold onto our little crumbs waiting for the successful conclusion. Maybe you and Lloyd can just spend time together as friends. Go for a walk with your dogs. Go out for coffee. Don't try to infer what the future might hold."

Tammy was right. I had to find a path through this middle time. Could Lloyd and I place our focus on one day at a time?

Thanksgiving morning, 2019. I awoke to six more inches of snow. The electricity had been turned on sometime during the night, but the satellite was covered in snow. That meant I had no phone or Internet. No way to communicate with Lloyd. I had planned to drive up to the trailer to cook our Thanksgiving meal, but I knew the Tacoma truck couldn't make it up the steep road of snow and slush, and even though my Jeep was a four-by-four, it was too low to the ground. I was stuck.

It was 6:45 a.m. Large flakes of snow fell to the ground, forming thick mounds. I had planned on meeting Lloyd at 10:00. I had to trust he'd figure it out if I didn't arrive at the designated time. I waited.

Around 8:00 a.m., it stopped snowing. I trudged out to the garage to get a ladder and lugged it over to the house. After I had leaned the ladder against the roof and climbed to the top step, I realized that I should have shut Poochie inside; she was running around the ladder at lightning speed. As a former rock climber, I had no fear of heights, but that little dog had me unnerved. I quickly brushed the snow off the satellite dish and slowly inched myself down to the ground.

When I returned to the house to try the phone, it worked. Relieved, I called Lloyd and told him my dilemma.

"You're right," he said. "The truck and the Jeep won't make it up this road. Branches are downed and the snow is deep. I'll drive to the house. We can have dinner there."

Lloyd had a Dodge Ram 4X4 with a Hemi engine, a truck with extra power for back roads. He could drive out, no problem.

Finally, a plan. After days without power, phone, or Internet, I wasn't sure if I'd be able to create a Thanksgiving spread, but with a working oven and stove top, preparations were smooth and easy.

Since there were only two of us, I had bought a turkey breast rather than a whole bird. Dinner was done by noon. We had decided on the earlier time so Lloyd could get back up the mountain before dark.

The sky was grey, the air frigid. At least the whiteness of snow brightened the world a bit. The cabin was clean and tidy, but there were no festive fall decorations. The smells of roasting turkey and strong coffee, pies on the counter (pumpkin for me and apple for Lloyd), and a crackling fire in the woodstove evoked a slight hint of festivity. Lloyd came to the house dressed in his usual attire: Levi's jeans, a flannel shirt, small hoop earrings, and work boots. I dressed in similar fashion: Levi's, a black sweater, beaded earrings, and house slippers. I'd put on clean jeans, but by the time Lloyd had arrived, they were already speckled with muddy dog prints.

During our meal, Lloyd chatted pleasantly. I tried to stay calm, holding down waves of grief. I feared my sadness might spill over and ruin our holiday dinner. My body felt robotic, tight, and controlled. I knew I had to talk to Lloyd, but speaking was hard. I waited until coffee and dessert. I tried not to cry, but tears tumbled out with the words.

"I'm struggling with the uncertainty in our marriage," I said. "I don't even know where home is anymore. Is it here, in our cabin, or is it in the trailer on the land? How do we stay married when we're living in separate places? You haven't stayed overnight in our home for over two months. If we live apart, we can be friends, but you may lose me as a wife if we don't spend more time together."

There were no romantic words in Lloyd's reply. Only this: "I understand."

Bringing Back the Light

While Lloyd and I struggled with our marriage, Jess and Jake settled into their FEMA trailer. The call came in early September. "Your FEMA trailer is ready. You can move in next week. Come to the FEMA office to pick up your keys and sign the contract." Because my sons had lived on the same parcel of property and were related, they shared a trailer. Our load was instantly lightened. Jess and Jake had a three-bedroom, two-bath, no-frills modular. We marveled at closets and drawers as if they had just been invented. There was a stove, oven, microwave, and refrigerator. All brand-new and shiny clean. The kitchen/living/dining area was huge. Annie danced in the big room. Marie spun in circles. Large windows brought in light. Layers of anxiety and loss due to the Camp Fire began to melt away.

My grandadughters' mother's trailer was identical to their dad's and located on the same gravel road. Annie and Marie spent weekdays with their mother and stepdad; Friday night through Sunday with Jake. School had started, and with it, a routine. Marie began to sleep through the night. She still had occasional nightmares, but she was more settled. Annie could run. No more crowded, camp-trailer living.

October. We had a birthday party for Jake in their new digs. Pizza baked in the oven. The scents of oregano and fresh baked crust gave the kitchen a birthday party smell. (Years of such gatherings at Chuck E. Cheese and Round Table Pizza had left a lingering impression.) After eating our greasy, gooey feast, Jake opened his gifts. Then, there was cheesecake and ice cream.

November was the month for our family's traditional outing to the pumpkin patch. The day was seasonably warm, the sky a brilliant blue. The earthy smells of horses and hay filled the air. Karen, Jake, Jess, Annie, Marie, and I rode around the farm in a hay wagon pulled by a tractor. We sipped cinnamon-spiced apple cider, tasted bites of pumpkin pie. The girls searched the fields to find the perfect pumpkins to take home. Later, the decorated pumpkins would sit on the wooden steps that led to the trailer.

In December, Karen bought her brothers a Christmas tree. The family spent the afternoon decorating the tree. Annie remembered "Jingle Bell Rock," the song she sang at the Christmas program at her elementary school in Paradise. The school was lost to the fire, but she recalled with enthusiasm the song-and-dance routine her class performed. The following week, I brought cookie cutters, sugar cookie mix, icing, and red-and-green sprinkles. The girls and I rolled out dough, cut it into trees, snowmen, and snowflakes. When the cookies were baked and cooled, we topped them with swirls of colored frosting and sprinkles. Later, Annie drew Christmas pictures of Santa, reindeer, and her family standing outside their home. We listened to Christmas songs on Marie's iPad. The house felt festive and light.

After they lost their homes in the fire and drifted for almost a year, we clung to these simple rituals that had turned their modest FEMA trailer into a warm and loving home. Yet, amid celebration, worry remained. FEMA offered the trailers for eighteen months, but the countdown began the day the Camp Fire was declared a national disaster. That meant the homes were available for only eight months. We hoped for an extension, and in the meantime, we savored every precious moment.

When I reflect on my life during that time, I see piles strewn across a floor: a massive load of grief and loss due to the Camp Fire, a pile of relief and gratitude for the FEMA home, a mound of messy moments from a broken marriage. Lingering uncertainties. Life was like an accumulation of chaos and bliss that I had assembled in the dark. How would I sort and stack the piles to form a cohesive whole? I waited for light.

Chapter Six
Winter 2019

Uprooted

Instead of light, I got ticks. It was early December and still no freeze. We had plenty of rain and several days of snow, but the temperature would not drop low enough to kill off the tiny black ticks that plagued the woods surrounding our yard. In a single day, I used my pointy-edged tweezers and pulled off nine ticks from my poor little dog. I was completely creeped out; my skin crawled, and my head itched. I felt bites all over my body, even though no ticks were embedded there.

Poochie did not get ticks when we were out at the trailer, where the dogs ran through thick brush and forest. Poochie's tick infestation came from the half-acre, wet, wooded yard at the house. Fed up and repulsed by the hordes of ticks, my sentiments towards my home began to change.

That night. Two o'clock in the morning. A misty full moon outside my window. Drained and worn out, I tried to sleep, but the dogs across the road barked on and on. I blamed the neighbors who kept their two dogs kenneled. The poor dogs were rarely out of their prison. Still... *I hate those dogs. Every damn night. Stupid neighbors. They shouldn't have dogs. God, I hate this neighborhood. Hate the road. The ticks. I hate it here.* I turned on my side, pulled the blankets up to my neck, placed a pillow over my ears. I felt displaced. Torn. Where was home anyway? The dogs continued to bark. I continued to whine. I liked it better on the property with Lloyd. I needed quiet. *I hate this house.*

I didn't really hate the house. It was small and comfortable, an eighty-year-old Forest Service home. Lloyd had painted each room a different color: yellow in the bathroom and kitchen, sage green in the bedroom, a rosy tan in the living room. Upstairs, one of the attic rooms was mint green, the other a soft yellow. Like the trailer, our cabin was also surrounded by trees, but neighbors were visible. When we moved into this home, the road was crumbled, cracked, and filled with potholes. Last summer, the state gave rural areas grants to pave their roads; the street in front of our home was layered with asphalt. I was horrified. The road was still narrow and winding, a typical undulating mountain road, but it was too conventional for my lifestyle. I wanted dirt, mud, layers of leaves.

I started staying out on the land with Lloyd more often. We were moving forward. Not just as friends, but as husband and wife. When I was out at the trailer, I was surrounded by forest. I marveled at the silky-smooth bark of the madrones, the red satin bark, and twisted limbs of manzanitas with their decorative reddish-orange berries. Cedars, mossy green oaks, and looks-like-Christmas toyon bushes, loaded with clumps of deep-red berries, all formed a circle around the clearing in front of the trailer. In the distance, a view of the rolling hills below. Lloyd and I awoke in the woods. No neighbors were seen, no road ran by the home. No ticks or barking dogs. The place was private, providing peace and calm.

I wanted to spend more time at the trailer, but the wet weather and rutted road often kept me out. Lloyd had to pick me up in the Dodge to drive me up to the land. I didn't want to depend on Lloyd. I liked my independence and felt uncomfortable asking for a ride, like I was some unlicensed adolescent. Until a year ago, I drove a heavy-duty Toyota Tundra 4X4. When the transmission finally gave out after more than three hundred thousand miles, Lloyd bought the Jeep.

"We really don't need another big truck," Lloyd had said.

And we didn't at the time. We were no longer living at five thousand feet elevation, driving hazardous roads on snow and ice. At first, I didn't like the Jeep: too low to the ground, a city car, a car for old ladies who didn't drive in mountains and mud. But it was a great vehicle, and the four-wheel drive came in handy when traveling through snow. Now, I wanted to sell it.

"If I'm going to spend time with you, I need a real four-by-four," I said. We were back to the same conversation we had begun a few months back. Do we sell the Jeep? What about the house? Do we keep it as a place where I can access the Internet and write? As a place to do laundry, store tools, take hot showers, and use later down the road when our bodies grow weaker with age? I couldn't grasp the idea of living in two places, as it was I who was uprooted and traveling back and forth between our two homes. For four months, Lloyd had stayed out at the trailer. Sure, he came by the house to help me cut wood. He pruned the fruit trees, put in a kennel for Poochie (who we now called Little Bit), but Lloyd no longer spent the night there. As I drifted between the house and the trailer, neither place felt like home. I had become the fragile surface roots of an oak, sensitive to change and pressure, ready to bring the tree crashing down at any moment.

The Rocking Chair

Lloyd bought me a rocking chair. An old cane-back chair, its wooden arms and legs worn smooth with a fine sheen. It was small and fit snugly in the trailer's tiny front room.

Back in September, when Lloyd began to fill the trailer with furnishings, he brought his favorite items from our house: ceramic Aztec sculptures, pink quartz and Brazilian crystals, carved miniature boxes, and antique oil lamps. He brought his Native-print Pendleton blankets. Later, he bought a small table-and-chair set, a bookcase for his books, and an eclectic mix of colorful dishes from the local thrift shop. Nothing in the trailer belonged to me. Before Lloyd bought the rocker, his great-aunt's straight-backed captain's chair filled the space. I understood Lloyd's connection to this family heirloom, but the chair was uncomfortable. I had mentioned in conversation how nice it would be to sit in a rocker. Lloyd's gift of the rocking chair was a pleasant surprise and the beginning of a space for me.

The day I got the rocker, the sun had been out for several days, and the muddy road into the land had dried. I could now drive the Tacoma truck onto the property, and even though I knew the dry weather wouldn't last, I was happy to have the freedom to come and go as I pleased. This gave me time to establish a place for myself. I had been using the smaller trailer as a sort of she-shed. I had made up a cozy bed for naps, hung up a few clothes in the closet, but that was all. The time had come to set down roots. I bought extra underwear and socks and put them in the built-in drawers. I set the table with writing supplies, stored personal belongings in the cabinets. I bought a propane heater and new battery lamps. There were empty bookshelves above the windows; I decided to bring books. In the physical realm, it was a start, but I still had a way to go to feel emotionally *home*.

Rains replaced the sun, and once again, I had to hitch a ride from Lloyd to get into the property. The lack of autonomy and living in two homes made me feel transient and unsettled. *This is stupid. Many people live in separate homes, living apart for work or other reasons. Why can' t I navigate living in two places with a more organic flow?*

During this time, Lloyd had said to me, "Take your time; let things unfold."

He was right. I liked my time alone at the house, liked the freedom to create my days any way I chose. I also enjoyed staying on the land with Lloyd, walking through the woods in the day, and in the evening chatting by the glow of oil lamps. But I felt vulnerable, uncertain about our future as a couple. *Fuck flow*. Our separation still hurt.

Lloyd was living the dream: his return to life off the grid in his last years. But while he was firmly planted in place, I traveled like a nomad. One day, I came back from three days out with Lloyd, unpacked my clothing, medications, and personal items, did the laundry, and put away the cold foods I had left in the cooler (the old propane refrigerator at the trailer needed to be replaced). I unloaded and stacked the oak firewood Lloyd had cut for me, started a fire in the now-very-cold house, and took a shower. I then checked my phone and email messages, as I didn' t have an iPhone or another way to get phone or Internet service when away from the house. Each time I returned from the trailer, it felt as if I had arrived home from a long camping trip. My living situation didn' t seem fair. I was repeatedly renesting. Was I expecting too much?

The next time I stayed on the land with Lloyd, I asked, "Why don' t you stay overnight at the house? You rarely leave the trailer."

He paused for a moment. "The trailer' s a sacred space for me. I feel safe here. I need the tranquility." He added, "I don' t want conflict in my life right now."

"It sounds like you' re saying you don' t want to be around people. Conflict is a part of living with others," I said.

Lloyd offered up a wry smile. "You' re right."

Lloyd was tired; he needed a reprieve. His life had been challenging—a traumatic childhood, new health problems, and my family's overwhelming needs after the fire. I understood his fatigue.

As I sat in the rocker, watching the sun turn the fallen leaves and trees into a brilliant orange, I thought about new ways to begin our story instead of trying to cobble together what once was. Lloyd and I both needed to make accommodations to heal our aging selves.

Chapter Seven
Winter 2020

Some Perspective

The ticks had spread throughout the foothills. Not only were they latching onto our dogs at the house and the trailer, but friends and neighbors had reported similar tallies: fifteen ticks per dog, each day. In the cold winter months, nymphs (a sort of teenage tick) were typically inactive. It was mid-January 2020, yet freezing weather hadn't fully arrived. Of course, the real issue was not ticks, but the mild temperatures and warm rains due to climate change. Hmmm...

Something clicked. I saw how my focus on my personal tick misery had created a blind spot. The ticks were just a symptom of something much larger: global warming. Was I also missing the big picture in my marriage? Was it really so important to meander between two rustic but comfortable households? I owned a home, while my own children and grandchildren still lacked home security. I had talked about this issue with Jess.

"We had our FEMA meeting today," Jess said. "They approved our housing contract through May 12th. We were told we may be able to rent the trailer after that date, but we don't know the rental cost. I can't focus that far ahead. I must take life day by day. Today, I got new tires on my truck; tomorrow, I'll do laundry. It's the only way I can get through this," he said.

"I'm relieved you have a bit more time at the FEMA trailer," I said. "It's good you're moving through this by living in the present. Future unknowns are so overwhelming."

Later, as I thought about my conversation with Jess, I realized I was overwhelmed by a fragile future. I had frequently spoken the phrase, one day at a time. It sounded so simple, but it was not my reality. Instead, my brain was brimming with what-ifs: What if it takes months to move out to the trailer with Lloyd? What if our marriage deteriorates? What if my sons lose their home? What if I can't sort and stack the mess? What if I lose control?

Whenever I felt unmoored, adrift in a sea of uncertainty, I immediately tried to grasp the situation. I tried to manage Lloyd's and my current living arrangements. I tried to hold my family together after the fire. What if I failed? Deep down, I knew I did not have total control over life experiences, but my mind wouldn't take notice. I examined, speculated, reflected, and contemplated ways to control not just my life, but the lives of those close to me. I thought I was helping.

My control habit was steeped in fear. I was afraid Lloyd would abandon our marriage. Before that, I feared my sons and granddaughters would be homeless after the Camp Fire. Before that, I was afraid of my declining physical health and emotional stability. Before that, it was Jake's addiction. He could overdose. Before that, Jess had a liver transplant at age thirteen. He was diagnosed with idiopathic cirrhosis of the liver at eight years old. This was before liver transplants were common. He could have died.

I thought about these fears as I was snow camping inside the house. Outside, the wind raged, and snow fell in thick drops. I was out of wood and down to my last emergency Enviro-Log. The snow had covered the satellite dish for the phone and Internet, so there was no service. The power had shut off again. *Shit.* I left my new propane heater at the trailer.

As the night sky darkened and the last waxed-cardboard log turned to ash, I took a camp light out to the porch, where my one-burner camp stove sat on a table. I placed a pot of canned chili on the burner. With some whole grain crackers from the cupboard, a hot meal was ready in minutes. After eating supper and washing dishes, I lounged on the couch with Little Bit. My clothes were snug and cozy. As usual, nothing matched: flowered print pajama pants; an old, white fleece camp shirt, complete with holes from campfire sparks; a blue/brown/orange Native-design robe; thick, fuzzy multicolored socks. Under dim camp lights, I settled in to read. An hour later, I went to bed.

For some, this situation might have been one of their what-if moments. What if there was an emergency and I couldn't dial 911? What if the food in the freezer spoiled and I had no funds to replace it? Could I manage to sleep through the frigid night? But I had memories. Snow camping in Mount Shasta, Mount Lassen, the Trinity Alps, Mount Whitney. My past experiences of creating a home in the snow allowed me to find comfort on an inky-black night. I did not fear darkness, cold, isolation, or rationing food. *Maybe I could fill my mind with good experiences instead of fearful ones from other areas in my life.*

When I awoke the next morning, I pushed my way out from beneath layers of warm blankets to begin my day. A cold, sooty ash was all that remained of last night's fire. Thankfully, the power had turned back on around 3:00 a.m. I took a hot shower and dressed for the hour-long drive to town to buy more emergency Enviro-Logs.

Outside, a wet, sloppy snow covered the ground. As I drove down the hill, snow melted into puddles of grimy slush, then eventually disappeared. By the time I reached the valley, the steel-gray sky had morphed into a mix of white cumulus clouds and sun. For now, the storm had passed, and even though the weather would remain unstable for some time, a calm settled inside me. I was not fearless, but I gave myself permission to let life unfurl through the uncertainty.

Ready or Not

As I was trying to let life happen, events were moving at a faster pace than I had planned. I wanted to live in a cinematic slow-motion flower bloom, ease into change. I wanted to sit on my moss-covered rock overlooking the meadow and soak in nature. I wanted more time for Lloyd and me to work on our relationship. And I did not want to make any life-changing decisions.

Just as I was beginning to adjust to living in the house on my own, our neighbor, Tom, who owned the homes and property on either side of ours, stopped his construction truck in our driveway. After we said hellos, he asked if I had a moment, so I invited him into our yard and opened the gate. I had been cleaning out the dusty, gravel-floored garage. My hair was in its usual messy ponytail, and my jeans were smudged with red dirt, but Tom didn't seem to notice. He was all business.

"I heard you and Lloyd were thinking of selling your house." Tom knew we had another piece of land, and he had noticed Lloyd's absence.

"Lloyd's been working on our other place," I said. "It still needs work to make it livable. But we have thought about selling the house in the future." *I'm not even sure I'm ready to live with Lloyd full-time. Could I give up my personal space?*

I wasn't trying to make a sale, but I stupidly told Tom he could call Lloyd to discuss it. Tom was delighted. His elderly father and mother were our closest neighbors. We couldn't see their house, but Tom's dad raised birds of all types. He had built a pond and birdhouses for his pheasants and other exotic birds next to our front yard, making mornings sound like a jungle. Tom had a cabin on the opposite side of our yard next to our orchard. Tom and his wife used that home as a weekend retreat and a place to stay when visiting his parents.

A few days later, Tom made an offer on our house. A good offer. Cash. We wouldn't need to deal with a realtor or pay for inspections. Lloyd was elated. His dream was evolving. He could live his elderly years off-grid and off the beaten track.

"It means you'll have to live with me," I said.

"I'd like that," Lloyd said. "As long as no other family members live with us."

There it was. Not that I wanted my grown children living in our home again or that they had any intention of living with us.

"They can visit," Lloyd assured me. "Maybe we can have Easter here."

I was hesitant. Lloyd was confident. With a huge grin that I hadn't seen for some time, Lloyd said, "It's all coming together."

In many ways, that was true. I had spent more time out on the property and had created a place for myself. Lloyd knew I hated clutter and preferred a sparse, easy-to-clean space, so he planned to store more of his belongings in the smaller trailer. He had begun to transform the screen room into a usable space, as an office or yoga room. Even before the sale offer, Lloyd was building *us* a home. And yet, it was difficult for me to accept Lloyd's request to limit family members to visits only. Life was too uncertain. When times were hard, families stuck together. At least that was how I was raised. Lloyd wasn't raised by a loving family. He had to make it on his own. His *pull yourself up by your bootstrap's* stance, even when your shoes were burnt in a fire, was not likely to change.

I had been working with my therapist on this issue and felt ready to speak to Lloyd, hopefully in a way that would leave him feeling validated, and a way in which my concerns would be heard. The following week, Lloyd and I had some time to talk. We were at the cabin. We sat at the kitchen table, the afternoon light streaming in through the large windows in our small dining area.

I took a deep breath. "This house sale is coming together rather quickly. I'm not sure if I'm ready for it," I said. "I wanted more time to work through some things. I can't promise you absolutes about turning away family members who may need our help. But we can discuss solutions together. That way, we can both be heard, and we can make compromises instead of rules."

Lloyd took a moment to collect his thoughts, sipped his coffee slowly. "I think I can do that," Lloyd said. "I just don't want decisions thrown at me."

"I don't either," I said.

After the Camp Fire, I hadn't been able to visualize any other option. Housing opportunities were scarce. I didn't want my family to live in tents in the Walmart parking lot.

Lloyd hadn't seen the traumatized families in the makeshift camp: people sleeping in their cars; others in tents, soaking wet from rivers of rain. I hadn't asked Lloyd his thoughts on my sons moving in. I simply said to them, "Come stay with us until FEMA opens up housing." I had no idea how our one-thousand-square-foot home could hold four adults and two children. No idea it would take almost a year for them to be placed in a temporary home.

"I just want some say if something comes up," Lloyd said.

It seemed doable. With my family now safe in FEMA trailers, life looked more hopeful. Both my sons were working and integrated into the Chico community. We had a reprieve, and with it, some time to heal. Our problems weren't instantly solved, but we were communicating and found value in compromise. Together, Lloyd and I made the decision to sell our house. We would live off-grid full-time.

The Hill

Lloyd had been living on the property for six months, and I was there several times a week, but we hadn't spent any time with the neighbors hidden in the woods on the hill. We had met a couple of the younger "farmers" who owned land nearby as we drove on our dirt road easement, but talk was limited to brief introductions. We were told we had a neighbor close to us, but months went by before we would get to know him. We had passed each other in our trucks a couple of times, stopped for a brief hello, and then we'd drive off.

As the weather warmed and the mud dried out, our nearest neighbor drove up to our trailer for a visit. In his sixties, Paul was tall and lean with shoulder-length gray hair. He wore sweatpants with holes, a flannel shirt, and a black vest. Paul's father had bought his land in the 1970s, and Paul had spent his spare time building a cabin there. It took twenty years, but by the time he retired, his cabin was ready. Paul was friendly and intelligent, and because he had spent years on the hill, he knew its history and current story.

Paul told us, "We're the only ones who drive in on this easement through the meadow." The *we* was Paul, Lloyd, and me. "Part of the road belongs to another neighbor, Mike, who owns the land to our west. There are about five homes on top of the hill, but they travel in from a different road."

Lloyd had seen that small cluster of homes once before, when he had decided to hike up the hill. Due to many dead-end trails, Lloyd wandered lost for hours, walking in darkness without flashlight or warm clothes. His day hike turned into a seven-hour ordeal. He made it home by following animal trails and crawling through thick manzanita brush and mud. Unfortunately, it was too dark to see much, and he had no idea where he was, so he couldn't establish an orientation of the land. We had a map of the lots surrounding us, but the layout was confusing.

A few days after Paul's visit, Lloyd and I saw Mike on the road as we walked our dogs. He was driving a four-passenger Kubota ATV with a truck bed. Mike stopped and introduced himself. He was tall with a sturdy build. In his fifties, he had short black hair and dark eyes. Mike offered to give us a tour of the properties he owned, so I walked the dogs up our driveway, while Lloyd and Mike followed behind in the ATV. I put the dogs in their kennel, then climbed in the vehicle.

Mike narrated as he drove, but we only heard bits of his talk, as I was in the back seat and Lloyd wasn' t wearing his hearing aids; still, we heard enough to put the pieces together. Mike owned a tractor and had recently cut the roads through his newly acquired properties. Mike also owned an older modular home that he had purchased fifteen years ago. His new property added about thirty acres to his original ten-acre parcel.

Mike was a motor-head: he had several vintage Harley-Davidsons, rode dirt bikes, and owned a mechanic shop. A few of the roads he cut were for dirt bikes. As we bounced along the rough trails, Lloyd turned his head towards me and said, "This is fun." I agreed. It was like riding through a Disney Adventure. We climbed up hills, drove down steep dips, and splashed through puddles. The morning sun filtered through the forest, and the damp earth smelled swampy. It *was* fun, but I worried about the noise we might hear while Mike was riding. There was a bright side: the roads Mike cut made for a quick way out to the main road in case of fire. Mike generously offered his permission for Lloyd and me to drive or walk his roads at any time.

During our ride through the woods, we saw the usual contrasting scenes found in rural forests: large holes in the ground from years-ago mining, old logging roads that ended abruptly, and heaps of trash left from former pot growers who had been busted and ousted from the land. I knew these types of sites well, but they always left me in a melancholy mood. How could people degrade the backwoods for monetary gain? I knew that for many, poverty was a factor. There wasn' t money for dump runs, and often, rusted old cars and demol-ished trailers were used for parts. Still, I could not imagine it reason enough to mar the landscape. Even though these blemishes were hidden behind brush and timber, I felt violated, as if someone had tarnished my home.

Mike interrupted my thoughts. "I plan to clean up these old trail-ers," he said. "Do you want to look at them?"

To my dismay, Lloyd said, "Sure!"

Lloyd had mentioned earlier our need for a refrigerator, and he believed that an old trailer was the place to score one. So, we made a stop to look inside one of the better trashed trailers. Rust and peeling paint crusted the outside. A moldy, mildewy smell greeted us when we opened the door.

"The refrigerator looks like it's in pretty good condition," Lloyd said.

Black mold and other undetermined smears spread across the inside of the fridge. "I don't want it," I quickly replied. "I wanted a clean refrigerator."

"I think it's too small," Lloyd told Mike.

I was relieved and thankful, knowing that once we sold our other home, we could afford a new propane refrigerator. I'm more of a minimalist than Lloyd, and hate clutter, but what home essentials we do have must be clean and good quality. Lloyd, on the other hand, loves thrift stores, anything recycled and a great deal.

After we viewed the refrigerator, Mike drove the ATV down our driveway and dropped us off. We said our goodbyes, then Mike rode back to his place.

I didn't need to worry about the sound of dirt bikes or an invasion of our privacy, as we didn't see our neighbors again for quite some time. Perhaps these first visits were a sort of interview so Paul and Mike could get a feel for their new neighbors. Like us, they preferred to be left alone. But there was also this: as Lloyd and I slowly moved our life and belongings onto the property that February of 2020, COVID-19 was spreading. Just three weeks after our neighbors' visits, the governor of California requested that all senior citizens over the age of sixty-five and those with chronic disease isolate themselves at home. Lloyd and I fit both categories.

Chapter Eight
Spring 2020

Hunkered Down

Mid-March. After a February completely devoid of rain, we finally saw strong winter winds, heavy showers, and even a bit of snow. As I looked out the trailer's glass slider, I saw that a light layer of white had covered the ground and draped the trees. A heavy mist blurred the distant view.

Before mandatory isolation and the closure of indoor restaurants, I had met with Jess and Karen at the bookstore café. Not one to order fancy coffee drinks, Jess drank his usual coffee with cream. Like Jess, Karen and I ordered our usuals: green tea for Karen, a steamy latte for me. Jess and I split a warm blueberry scone. We talked about the coronavirus.

"You better get toilet paper," I told Jess. "I just went to Walmart, and the shelves were completely empty." I had heard about toilet paper hoarding but was shocked to see it.

"The school district is talking about closing the schools and using online instruction," Karen said.

She taught at a hybrid school: the students were in the classroom two days a week and on independent study the other three days.

"Our school is set up for online instruction," Karen said. "I hope they make the change soon." Karen was worried about the close contact of the classroom environment.

The visit was brief, as Karen had another appointment, and I had planned to visit Jake, Annie, and Marie. We gave each other hugs. We didn' t know it then, but that would be our last contact for a long while.

After a quick stop at the grocery store, I went to visit my grand-daughters. Marie and I sat smooshed side by side in a beanbag chair. I read to her while she interjected comments and made sound effects. I brushed her messy blond hair away from her face. She was beautiful: dark-blue eyes surrounded by thick, black lashes; rosy cheeks; dimples. Sitting close to Marie in the sunny room made it easy to forget how our futures might change.

While Marie and I read, Annie rode her bike with her dad, Jake. When Annie stepped through the door, her face was flushed.

"Grandma," she said, her eyes wide with delight. She rushed into the room and wrapped her arms tightly around me, her limbs icy from the cold wind.

I wanted to sit on that chair, smothered between my two grand-daughters, forever. I had heard rumors of a state lockdown, a stay-in-place directive, but momentarily, I put it out of my mind. I wanted to stay present, hold the moment.

A few days later, the governor made the announcement. Only essential travel would be allowed. Lloyd and I both canceled all non-essential trips off the mountain. Lloyd canceled a tattoo appointment. I had stopped going to my weekly therapy sessions and bimonthly writing group. I could no longer visit my family. Our only travel was to our cabin home to wash laundry, shower, and collect foods from the refrigerator and stocked cupboards.

Lloyd and I were completing our move from the cabin to our off-grid trailer. We had a thirty-day escrow, and time was ticking fast. We spent days sorting and packing our belongings. Some items went into a storage unit, others to the local thrift store, and the rest was moved to the property. We made numerous runs to the dump. These activities kept us going, kept our minds busy, and kept us isolated.

Like Lloyd, I was now living full-time at the trailer. As the packing and moving subsided, we hunkered down on the land.

April. Stress was a trigger for my chronic fatigue. I tried not to worry about the spread of COVID-19, but I couldn't help being concerned about Jake, who was still working, delivering organic coffee to grocery stores throughout several counties. I worried about Marie, who would miss daily learning at her school that specialized in supporting autistic children. I wondered how Annie, at ten, would fare without her friends.

Mornings were hard. My body burned with stinging pain, like I had swallowed bees. My bones ached, felt heavy as Kettlebells. It seemed impossible to lift my weight, but after six years of living with these autoimmune symptoms, I knew that if I could get up, the physical movement and mental distraction would ease the pain. So, I heaved myself out of bed, made coffee, and checked in with family and friends through email. By mid-morning, my joints felt fluid, my limbs lighter. I was moving less robotically, more humanlike.

Still wearing my flannel pajama bottoms and a T-shirt, I pushed my stocking feet into black Sorel boots, zipped myself into a fleece jacket, and walked out the door, Little Bit beside me. We walked down the dirt road under an arbor of dense forest. The birds sang their morning songs in the trees above us as if it were an ordinary day. We wandered down to the open meadow where the trees parted, and the sky loomed large. The air was brisk. Clouds scattered across the sky, giving a hint of the afternoon rain to come. The redbud trees were in full bloom. Splashes of violet mixed with brilliant spring greens. Puddles of water glowed silver in the sun. Little Bit darted across the meadow, dashed through the trees.

Among nature, relief shrouded me with the illusion of safety, but I couldn't shake the sadness of loss. Even though I talked to my family on the phone and emailed friends, I longed for the comfort of closeness: my sons' warm hugs, the scent of my grandaughters' freshly shampooed hair, my daughter's bright smile. The life we once lived had been suspended in air. As I walked along the seasonal creek towards home, I marveled at the clusters of delicate pink shooting stars, their nodding petals, their yellow noses pointing to the ground, the way their slender stems pushed through the swampy marsh, their sweetness just beginning.

Dancing on the Radio

"I'm dying." It was my eighty-eight-year-old mother on the phone. "Why do you think you're going to die?" I asked.

"Dorothy wrote me a letter to say goodbye," she said. Dorothy was our next-door neighbor many years ago. My mother and Dorothy had kept in touch by writing letters. "Dorothy's the same age as me. She said we'd probably both die soon, so she wanted to say goodbye."

My mother talked in a slow, halting way. Often, her sentences were left dangling. "All my friends are dead. Even the wives."

My mother had maintained lifelong friendships with a group of women who attended high school together in the late 1940s. Most of my mother's friends had been widowed years earlier, but my father, at eighty-nine, was still alive. "It's just Don and Lavona now," she said. My mother was not sad. She spoke in a matter-of-fact tone.

"Well, I've had a long life," she said. "I was thinking about all of the places we've lived. And that's a lot of places."

"You're right, Mom. You've lived a long life and in some nice places," I said.

Like my mother, I wasn't sad about her potential death. I worried more about her debilitating pain, her constant fatigue, her memory loss.

I hadn't seen my mother in six months. I was scheduled to fly to Southern California for a visit in January, but my mother had fallen on her bathroom floor. Her third fall. There were no broken bones this time but bruising and a past hip replacement had my father worried.

"Maybe you can come down after your mom heals," he said. I canceled my flight and had planned to make a trip south in March.

The summer before, I had visited my parents in their Laguna Niguel home. My mother dressed fashionably in white capris, a black-and-white scoop-necked shirt, beaded earrings. Her speech was spunky. Her older sister, Ramona, was visiting, too. Ramona also dressed in capris, but her look was more conservative. A pink-and-white-striped shirt, a gold cross necklace. Only a year apart, my mother and her sister had inherited my grandfather's high cheekbones and thin lips, but my mother was slender, while her sister was round and matronly.

Ramona and my mother told stories of growing up in Arkansas. Hearty laughter floated through the house as they told tales about their youth on the Snake River. How they'd hang dead water moccasins in the trees to scare people, or the time my mother and Ramona had *danced* on the radio.

"The radio announcer interviewed me," my mother said. "I learned something about myself. He mentioned my dark eyes and how they contrasted with my white-blond hair. I had never thought of that before," she said.

I wasn't sure how one tap-danced on the radio, but I assumed the tapping was heard on the audio. It was the only time Ramona had ever danced.

"I was upset because I had to sing the boy part," Ramona said.

She wore a tuxedo made of black oilcloth, while my mother wore a frilly dress, as she was the more experienced dancer. We all laughed at the silliness of dancing on the radio. Ramona found it hilarious that she was so mad about wearing a boy outfit, realizing now that no one had seen her.

On that summer afternoon, my mom appeared healthy. Her walk had slowed since her hip replacement several years earlier, and her memory occasionally lapsed, but her conversation was lively, her smile radiant.

I couldn't get a flight south in March, as we were in the midst of the pandemic. The coronavirus had already spread illness and death throughout California's densely populated coastal areas, including my parents' hometown. I canceled my plans again.

While the coronavirus kept us under shelter-in-place orders, my mother's health continued to spiral downward. Over a period of six weeks, I had received email updates from my sister, Kimi. In each letter, the reports became dire: The doctor said Mom was extremely fragile and needed twenty-four-hour care; Mom's cancer was back, and it was more aggressive; they took Mom to the emergency room due to major swelling but were not sure of the cause yet. In her last email, Kimi wrote, "As soon as the airlines are back in business, I think you should book a flight. You need to see Mom ASAP."

My flight was originally booked to arrive in Long Beach, Kimi's hometown in Los Angeles County, the California epicenter for COVID-19. Infection rates were still increasing. At the time of Kimi's message in April, LA County had averaged forty-four deaths per day. I wouldn't be on an airplane any time soon. Like Dorothy, I wondered if I would see my mother again.

Love You More

"Gramma, you come to my house today?" Marie asked.

"Grandma can't come over for a while. She might get sick. I miss you, Marie," I said.

We were six weeks into our shelter-in-place order, and I had finally figured out how to make a videophone call with WhatsApp. I didn't have Wi-Fi; neither did Jake. It took some time to find a messaging service that would connect directly to our cellular devices.

"She asks the same question every weekend," Jake said. "She doesn't understand why you can't come."

I was shaken with sadness at this news, but how could I convey a pandemic to a six-year-old autistic child? I mustered up a smile.

"I can see you on my phone, Marie. Can you see me?"

"Your face is red," she said. She was right; my face was lit with sunburn. "You come over?" she asked again.

My insides went hollow. "As soon as I can, I'll come see you," I said.

Marie left the phone briefly to retrieve her new toy, a small black-and-white Sonic the Hedgehog bendy, a flexible action figure.

"His name is Shadow," Marie said. Shadow was Sonic's rival. Marie twisted its limbs, creating some sort of superhero pose. Marie and Annie were crazy about Sonic the Hedgehog video games and toys.

"Sonic is fast, like me," Annie said. At ten, Annie was a strong runner. And quick. "I have Tails and Knuckles" (Sonic's friends). Annie was now on the video call, too. Her long hair fell over her face as she moved in and out of the screen, picking up various action figures to show me. My iPhone screen was small, and the video repeatedly froze, but watching Annie sweep her hair behind her ear and Marie flutter her small hands as she spoke was like witnessing a small miracle. I wanted to reach into the phone and pull them close, and even though that was not possible, I sensed a contentment I hadn't felt in weeks.

When Annie and I concluded our call with our usual "love you more," I turned off the phone. Sitting in the sun in my old camp chair, with the heat softened by a cool breeze, my world flushed with life. Little Bit chased lizards in a brush pile; Jackson lay sleeping in the soft spring grass. I could hear Lloyd's hammer tapping as he pounded nails into boards that would soon become a new porch. The daffodils were gone now, but silky, orange poppies and spires of purple lupine bloomed across the hillsides.

Magic and Morons

They came out from the woods each evening. I never saw them, but I heard their voices, the pounding of nails, the whir of a screw gun. At dusk, a loud, grating mechanical sound filled the darkness. I was irritated by the sound, but eventually, the wind stirred the trees to life. Branches creaked and leaves shook. The wind's strength diminished the motorized noise and muffled voices. By the time the sky turned black, only the wind was heard, a mere whisper, then silence.

I liked to think of elves, magical forest creatures living in hollowed-out trees, hiding from humans in the day, venturing out in the darkness to plant gardens and build greenhouses. The reality was different. My elves were pot farmers, and the machine sounds were large generators for greenhouse warmth and lighting. For several weeks, the farmers worked diligently to bring their clones, clippings from another plant, to life. As the days grew longer and the sun blazed hotter, natural light replaced the grow lights. The generators ceased. Screw guns were no longer needed to shore up the greenhouses. They stood strong and solid. Quiet returned to the forest.

On our homestead, Lloyd had planted gardens, too. Life was evident everywhere. Snow peas popped out of the ground days after planting. Delicate carrot tops pushed from the earth. Tomatoes, planted in large fabric grow bags, grew thick and strong in their cages. In the meadows, grasses grew tall. Brambles of prickly blackberries, once dry and brittle, trailed along the banks of a small stream.

There was also the slick, deep-red leaves of poison oak, some just beginning to turn green. I was careful to avoid touching the plants, but my forearms were covered in a red, scaly rash, as Little Bit wandered through the poisonous shrubs with abandon. Her furry coat, covered in the plant oils, had rubbed against my arms.

Other life-forms thrived. Tiny frogs found their way into the wet areas throughout the property. One little frog lived in the outhouse between the toilet seat and lid until I caught it and tossed it in the grass. Large jackrabbits dashed about, with Little Bit in hot pursuit. Raccoons screeched, snarled, and purred in the night. The spider world exploded. Every day, I swept out daddy longlegs and cobwebs from the outhouse and the screened-in bedroom. Mosquitoes pierced my skin with their tiny straw mouths. Pink, itchy blotches covered my arms, shoulders, and feet. But these were minor obstacles, relieved by hours of soaking in the sensations of the forest.

I wanted to hold onto these magical woods, bathe in their sweet forest fragrance, but we lived in a time of contrasts. Life with

COVID-19 was stressful. Small trips to the grocery store or the local medical clinic took energy I didn't always have. My mind was on overload: wear a mask and gloves, don't touch my face, wipe down truck door handles and the steering wheel. Wash my hands with hot soapy water when the gloves come off. I worried when I touched my face, scratched my nose. I worried when someone unmasked stood too close.

Even though we lived in a small community with only a handful of coronavirus cases, staying safe felt like a chore. Many people in rural communities believed their distance from cities kept them safe, so they frequently defied stay-at-home orders, stood too close to others, and rarely wore masks. It pissed me off. I'd bite my lip to keep from yelling, "Selfish bastards."

My sweet nature-girl persona unraveled. I struggled to find balance. The pandemic surged around the world, yet here, in this beautiful land, ignorant morons surrounded me. My forest life was calming, but I had to walk in two worlds. As an introvert, I'd happily stay home, but we needed food, treats for the dogs, propane, and medications. Living in complete seclusion wasn't possible.

And not everyone was a moron. I sometimes found magic in people. Driving out on the dirt road to pick up my medications at the local clinic, I pulled over when I saw Julian's truck. He was one of my night elves. He had soft, shoulder-length brown hair, a smattering of freckles across his nose. A kind face. He was in his early thirties.

"Are you and Lloyd settled in?" he asked.

"Just about," I said. "We just signed papers for the sale of our old house, so we're almost there."

"If you need any help, give me a call," he said. "We should all get together for a potluck sometime."

"That would be great," I said.

Julian returned a smile. I knew his offers were sincere, but I also knew I wouldn't see him for a while. Our paths didn't cross that often; still, Julian and the other elves had given Lloyd and me their phone numbers in case we needed anything. That caring gesture was enough. I drove away, filled with Julian's sweetness, enchanted by his youthful optimism and the clumps of yellow iris that bloomed along the dusty roadside.

Chapter Nine
Summer 2020

Little Moments

A dull morning. Tired and groggy, I forced myself out of bed, rallying when I thought of steaming coffee made in the French press. As the beverage steeped, I poured real half-and-half and two teaspoons of stevia into my cup. A luxury. The bittersweet taste awakened my senses. I drank it slowly, relishing the moment as I waited for a phone call from Kimi. She would soon update me on the news from my father's recent appointment.

For months, there had been no diagnosis for my eighty-nine-year-old father's symptoms. A painful red rash had developed on his face. Bleeding lesions left him unable to shave. Dried blood crusted on his beard. He had been to three dermatologists and had received topical creams. His skin bruised purple. His face swelled. A new dermatologist gave my father a different medication that cleared up his face, but his blood work revealed another problem. The dermatologist sent my father to an oncologist. We now waited for word on probable cancer.

The call came in the afternoon. "Dad has stage four angiosarcoma, a rare and aggressive form of cancer," Kimi said.

Angiosarcoma cancer forms in the blood vessels and typically begins in the head and the neck. My dad's cancer had already spread to his shoulders, down his arms.

"Dad can try radiation. The oncologist said it might give him a bit more time, but it might not help at all. The doctor said Dad has four to six months, but Dad's determined to outlive Mom, so he may try the radiation treatment. Dad and I told Mom about the cancer.

She understood the seriousness of his disease. I just hope Dad won't suffer too much," Kimi said.

I knew my father wanted to live, as he believed my mother needed him to care for her, but truthfully, she had more emotional strength than he realized. Her health was deteriorating, but she still had attitude and a sense of humor. I thought about the last time I spoke to my mother on the phone.

"What are you doing today?" I asked.

"I'm just lying-in bed like an old bag," she said. I smiled at the image.

"It sounds like you have company," I said. I knew Kimi was visiting and could hear my father's loud voice in the background.

"Kimi's here with her new boyfriend. Dad's telling him stories. I'm glad they're here. I'm tired of hearing the same ol' tales." My mother always found a sliver of the positive in the simplest moments.

I shifted from the memory and focused on the current phone call. "Dad has another appointment next week with the cancer treatment team," Kimi said. "I'll call you when we know more."

I thanked her and hung up the phone. As I sat at the tiny kitchen table, I looked out the window. A mist of clouds floated through the trees. Raindrops hit the ground, and the fragrance of the dampened earth filled me. I felt relief. We now had a name for my father's disease. A time frame for living.

A few days later, Ramona called. She had just spoken to my mother. Ramona told me that my parents were outside, sitting together on the patio, listening to music. The image was tangible. I had seen it many times before. The sky, deep blue and clear. A view of the ocean and a breeze tasting of salt. *Their* songs spinning on the CD player. Johnny Mathis, Elvis Presley, Frank Sinatra. Favorites from the late 1940s and 1950s. They weren't worried about the future; instead, they reminisced as the songs carried them away.

The Undulating Hills

The days were wavy. The sloping ups and downs weren't as sharp or abrupt as the loss and destruction brought upon my family during the Paradise Camp Fire, but still, it was hard to catch a foothold. Heat melted my brain. My elderly parents were dying. My children and granddaughters were still in temporary FEMA homes. And we were five months into the COVID-19 pandemic.

July. A heat wave. Without air-conditioning, I simply deflated. When the temperature reached 98 degrees, my brain was unworkable: I couldn't think, couldn't read, couldn't write. My entire existence was focused on cool-down action: drink water with ice, mist my body with a spray bottle, cool my neck and face with wet rags, dip my feet in a tub of cold water, hose down clothing until soaking wet, jump in the outdoor shower every hour. Repeat. In the evening when the forest shadows returned, I would make a light dinner, wash dishes. An entire day would go by without any other accomplishments.

Fortunately, the heat waves weren't a constant. Some days, the temperatures were in the low eighties, with breezes. On those days, I was a force: I washed and line-dried laundry, swept and mopped floors, dusted the trailer and wiped it clean. In the evening, I wrote and read. It felt good to have an active mind, a moving body.

During this time, down in Southern California, my sisters had their hands full caring for my parents. Even though my mother now had a full-time, live-in caregiver, it took an all-hands-on-deck approach to keep my parents comfortable and living in their own home. Kimi drove my father to doctor appointments. My sister Sandi's son, Jon, took my mother to her appointments. My niece, Kimi's daughter, did the grocery shopping. In addition, there were numerous trips to the emergency room.

After one trip to the ER, my mother was admitted to the hospital due to severe edema. I spoke with Sandi on the phone.

"Mom's doctor called me this morning. He said that her ultrasound showed Mom has cirrhosis of the liver. I guess you can get it just from being older. It causes all the same signs as congestive heart failure, so they really don't think she has that now. Her liver is the primary cause of the swelling, confusion, and sleeping. The doctor said that Mom's memory is good. She's mentally strong."

"That's encouraging," I said. "Is Mom home yet?"

"Kimi's taking Mom home from the hospital this afternoon, as there's not much more they can do. The good news is her swelling is down and her breathing is much better," Sandi said.

"How's Dad holding up?"

"Poor Dad. He went to the emergency room on Friday, and all he was doing was putting a small Popsicle in his mouth, and that caused an artery to bleed. Yesterday, he was afraid to eat or go to the bathroom for fear that he would bleed again. Fortunately, Olivia, their caregiver, made soup, and he ate something. I don't know what happened this morning, but the bleeding started again. He's back in the ER."

"I wish I could help," I said.

I wanted to support my parents and sisters, but Sandi and my parents lived in Orange County, Kimi in LA County. In April, when LA County had averaged forty-four coronavirus deaths per day, it was jaw-dropping news. By July, the numbers were staggering. The death rate had ticked up, with 3,534 lost lives. I still held my airline tickets to Long Beach, but flights were canceled.

"I'll have to wait longer before I try to reserve airline tickets," I said. "We'll see how things look in the fall."

My words fell flat. I doubted the virus would diminish anytime soon, and I wasn't certain my parents would last through the fall.

A week after my mother got out of the hospital, my father had already made three more trips to the emergency room due to bleeding. As I worried about my dad, other little fires ignited.

Karen called. "Hi Mom," she said. "Are you holding up in the heat?"

"I'm pretty miserable, and I broke out in a horrible rash."

Karen's voice cracked. "Mom, I don't like you living so far out, without air-conditioning, and the road..." Her words broke; she started to cry.

"I'm okay. You don't need to worry about me," I said.

I didn't mention the blowout I had on our dirt road earlier that day, how I had to walk a mile home. Lloyd drove back and changed the tire, putting on the spare. We ordered new, beefed-up, badass tires, so we were set.

The real reason for her tears was soon revealed. "Somebody ran a red light and totaled Dad's car. He's okay, but the car was all he had left from the fire. Why can't he just have some peace?"

Karen was right. It had been twenty months since the Camp Fire, almost two years. And yet. The dead and dying trees were still not removed from her father's property. He didn't have enough money to get a loan for even a tiny modular, and now, he would have to put what money he had saved into a vehicle. The insurance money would not be enough for a reliable car.

"He wants so little," Karen said. "But he can' t even get that."

I thought of my ex-husband, Craig. Like me, he was a minimalist. A trailer on his half acre in Paradise was all he wanted, a place where he could walk his dogs in peace. But rather than moving forward and settling down into a home of his own, at seventy-four years old, he was stuck in a FEMA trailer. It would take another year before a house in Paradise would be built.

"I know this is really a difficult time right now. And the constant worry about the virus must be hard. We' re going through another wave of collective grief," I said to Karen.

I thought, too, about my sons, still in a FEMA trailer, with rent soon due that was more than their combined income could carry. Would FEMA evict them during a pandemic? My sons sent a letter with copies of pay stubs showing their wages, but there was still no word on a reduced rent. FEMA was asking $1,600 a month for a trailer on a patch of gravel and weeds.

"We' ll get through this," I said. I had no idea how. Karen and I talked a bit more and hung up.

Later that afternoon, she sent me a text. "A neighbor is loaning Dad an old Honda. At least he can get groceries now. Dad said he still has the river and the birds where he can walk his dogs."

A good omen.

Gray

The sky was smoky haze. Fires raged around us. Ninety-five hundred acres to the east; twenty-four thousand acres north. Closer to home, spot fires of thirty-five, forty, one hundred acres flared. Planes and helicopters flew above us, setting my nerves on edge. Heat and wind ravaged the days.

I wanted brilliant blue, a sky contrasted with forest greens and golden hills. Vibrant color lifted my mood. Without it, I had nothing to grasp. Nothing to prevent the burning sting in my eyes, nose, and throat. Nothing to shore up a sense of hope. Summer had become my nemesis. Sweltering heat attacked my body, made the air hard to breathe. Red dust set me coughing and covered my clothes; my skin felt like chalk.

My mother was back in the hospital.

"Your mother is at the end stages of life. Her kidneys, liver, and heart are shutting down. That's why her edema is so bad, why her blisters pop and bleed. There's no cure. Her best option now would be hospice. A nurse can come to her home two days a week, and they will be on call 24/7."

Kimi sent this news to me in a text. Hospice sounded like a good option, as my mom would be home with my dad. Their caregiver, along with the nurses, could treat my mother's wounds and provide pain management. This would give my parents some peace.

With my mother a bit more settled, I had planned another video call. I imagined telling my mother how much she meant to me, how much she was appreciated and loved. Maybe share a few precious stories.

Sandi and Kimi were with my mother to help with the call. We had intended to connect in the late afternoon, but the call came early. It was Sandi on the line.

"Dad started bleeding again this morning, and by the time Kimi and I arrived, we had to call 911. We thought we'd better call you before the ambulance comes. Here's Mom."

Sandi handed my mom the phone, but my mother didn't understand how to use the video. I saw only pieces: curlers in her hair, her robe, and eventually, part of her face; but she saw me. Our conversation was confusing. My phone froze, and I couldn't understand my mother's words.

She told Kimi, "I don't know what to say."

Hearing those words broke my heart. "I love you, Mom," I said.

"I love you, too."

"I see your hair is in curlers. Are you going out?" I teased.

"Yeah, but I don't think I'm coming back. Every night I go to bed thinking I won't wake up, but every morning, here I am." A twist in my stomach. I tried to hold back tears, but sadness turned to quiet weeping.

"I wish I was with you, Mom." My mom said something in reply, but I couldn't understand her words. The phone froze again.

"You're the best mom ever. You're beautiful."

Mom, with a hint of a smile, said, "You lie, you lie, you lie."

"Mom, you'll always be beautiful."

She was dazzling. Petite. High cheekbones, dark-brown eyes with arched eyebrows. For years, bleached blond hair, but now, a soft silver. But it was my mother's character that was most delightful. She had a sassy sense of humor, was easygoing and empathetic, and she carried herself with quiet strength.

Sandi and Kimi appeared in the video screen. "The ambulance is here. Sorry to cut the conversation short. We'll try again soon."

Later, Kimi would tell me that when my mother saw me on the video, she pressed the phone to her heart, then kissed the phone, as if she could kiss me.

After the call, I felt hollow. The coronavirus was surging in Southern California; how would I say goodbye to my mom? In our once-normal world, I would have flown down to be with her. I would hug her, hold her hand, or sit quietly next to her, listening to her breathe. Instead, I felt trapped in a gray fog, separated from my family by hundreds of miles.

A few days later, the wind shifted. Color returned: a cobalt sky, fluffy, white-sheep clouds. A chance of thunderstorms. My circumstances didn't change, but I felt lighter.

Kimi called. "If you want to see Mom, you'll need to get down soon. She's getting weaker each week."

I tried calling the airlines again. This time, I was told I couldn't get a reservation until after November. "My mother's in hospice. I need to get to Long Beach in the next few weeks." My voice sounded too high. I was desperate.

"Let me see what I can find," the customer service person said. "Can you hold?"

I said yes and waited for five minutes. Listened to her tap away on her computer. No relaxing background music to soften the mood. Her voice came back on the line. "There are no available reservations until after November, and your tickets are only good through October. The airline has canceled all flights to Long Beach."

What the fuck?

"That's too late. Can I get a refund?" She put me on hold again.

"The airline will send you an email about your options." She hung up. I never received said email.

I had paid for two tickets but had to let it go. I tried another airline, the only one that still traveled from Sacramento to Long Beach. I bought a ticket for the following week.

Although I had discussed travel with my doctor, who gave me the okay to fly, I felt conflicted. I was thrilled at the thought of seeing my mother, saying a real goodbye. But I was frightened.

Shit, I' m going to LA County, where the virus is exploding. And on a plane. Thank God for Xanax, but what if someone sits close to me? I' ll be around crowds. What if the governor decides on a lockdown and I get stuck there? What if I get sick?

I tried to reason with myself. The airline assured me capacity was cut by one-third. I should have plenty of space. The airport was small, and Kimi would pick me up. I would only be there a few days. I would socially distance, wear my mask, wash my hands.

Who was I kidding? I was worried sick, but if I didn' t see my mother, I would regret it later. I was living in the gray. A place of uncertainty, where life could shift at any moment.

Unexpected

Late July. The shift came a few days after I had made my flight plans. Kimi called me on the phone.

"I saw Dad on Saturday. His face was swollen, and he said he was coughing up blood. I tried to persuade him to go to the emergency room, but he refused. At 5:00 this morning," (a Monday), "he was rushed to the ER. They admitted him into the hospital. He' s bleeding in his brain. The doctor is running more tests, but right now, they don' t expect him to live more than a few days."

Kimi told me that she had asked the doctor if Dad might make it through Friday, the day I would arrive. The doctor told Kimi she would know more after the test results were in.

No more news came that Monday. The doctor assured Kimi that our father was comfortable and being well cared for, but he was grumpy. How my dad continued to talk while his brain bled in two places was incomprehensible. Even the doctors were amazed. For four days, my dad stayed in the hospital. Due to the pandemic, no one in the family was allowed to visit, but on Wednesday of that week, Sandi and Kimi met with one of his doctors.

"We' re sending him home for palliative care. He may live another week or two, but he' s not the same man he was before he came in. He' s very weak, and he won' t be able to get out of his hospital bed. He can't walk, and he no longer has control of his bowels," the doctor said.

"Does my dad understand this?" Kimi asked.

Just the day before, she had talked with my dad on the phone. He told her he wanted to go home, sit in his own chair, and watch television. He thought he could still walk with a cane and get his favorite snack, chocolate pudding, from the refrigerator. Use the bathroom on his own.

"We'll be sending in a social worker to discuss his situation."

The following day, my dad called Kimi. He repeated what the social worker had told him. He was still grumpy about his circumstances, but he understood the seriousness of his deteriorating health. He would be sent home Friday, the day I would arrive.

On Thursday, my sisters drove to my parents' home. They rearranged the living room furniture to make room for his hospital bed. The living room was my father's man cave: he had a large flat-screen TV and his favorite chair with an end table for snacks. Paintings of seaside scenes hung on the wall. My mother had her hospital bed in the den off the kitchen, a bright, sunny room with large sliding doors that opened to roses and geraniums, a view of the ocean. A green lawn covered the large yard. A pergola offered shade. On August first, a Friday afternoon, I arrived in Long Beach, where I spent the night with Kimi.

The next morning, Kimi and I picked up Sandi and drove to visit my parents. We entered through the backyard so we wouldn't disturb my father, as the hospice nurse was with him. We opened the sliding door. My mother was resting in her recliner, eyes closed. I sat in the wheelchair next to her, held her hand. Her fingernails had been polished bright red. She wore her gold wedding ring with the green emerald, a gift from my father after fifty years of marriage. She wore a cotton nightgown printed with tiny purple flowers and with lace around the neck—not her style. Just last summer, she still dressed in her leopard- or zebra-print blouses, Levi's capris, earrings that dangled. But she looked well. The swelling in her legs had subsided. Her white hair, now soft and thick, had grown longer. I kissed her cheek.

"Hi Mom," I said.

She turned her head and looked at me, a spark in her dark-brown eyes. She smiled. I stroked her hair.

"I've missed you, Mom. How are you today?"

"I'm tired. Not sleeping well. I'm turned around."

My mother's caregiver, Olivia, explained that she had been staying awake at night and sleeping in the daytime.

I kissed her forehead. She closed her eyes. "Rest awhile, Mom. I'll go see Dad."

In the living room, my dad was propped up on pillows in his hospital bed. His head was wrapped in a stretchy beige bandage. The gauze circled his chin, and the ends were tied together in a knot on top of his head. He still had his white mustache. He wore a brown, print hospital gown. His bed faced the television and the large front-room window. The white blinds on the window were opened slightly, giving the room a soft light. My dad saw me. A hint of a smile.

"Hi Kan," he said. Kan was his nickname for me. "Did you just get down?"

I told my dad about my flight the day before. He greeted my sisters, then veered off in a long rant about the air conditioner.

He gesticulated with his right arm as he spoke. "When I came home last night, the house was hot. The air was off for days. I called Ozzie" (my dad's longtime friend) "to get Brian's number. Brian's a friend of Ozzie's, and he had worked on the AC before," my dad said.

"Turns out both the heater and AC weren't working. Brian replaced the thermostat."

Holy shit. My dad had cancer throughout his body, his brain was bleeding, and he was giving us a long monologue about how he had gotten the air conditioner fixed the night he came home from the hospital. He couldn't get out of bed, but he had made phone calls and worked out the details to get the house cool and comfortable.

We talked a bit more, my hand on his shoulder as I stood by his bedside. I could tell my dad was tiring, so I kissed his cheek and told him to get some rest, and my sisters and I went to the kitchen where we prepared lunch. Olivia made my mom a plate of Wheat Thins with cottage cheese and strawberry jam. My mother, now awake, carefully picked up each cracker with two red fingernails. Always a slow eater, she daintily ate her crackers one at a time.

The day was pleasant. My mom rested as my sisters and I shared stories, but she wasn't sleeping. Every now and then, she would throw her two cents in as we talked. We spent most of our day talking with my dad, swapping memories about growing up with a football coach as a father.

"Remember when we spent the summers in the weight room? We climbed the ropes and tumbled on the mats," I said. This was back in the late 1950s. My sisters and I were probably some of the first girls to hang out in a gym. "Remember when Kimi climbed the goal post on the football field and fell?"

"I remember," my dad said. "I'm glad I had you girls, as I had to spend my days with forty boys." He spoke enthusiastically about his coaching years, his ball players, his winning teams.

By late afternoon, my dad began to experience sharp pains. At first in his feet, then down his legs. As we finished our visit, my dad said, "You three girls were the best thing that ever happened to me."

The last words spoken to his daughters.

Sandi, Kimi, and I left my parents' home around 5:00 p.m. Later that night, as my dad's pain increased, Olivia called hospice. Two nurses came to the house to begin morphine. Olivia called Kimi.

"Two hospice nurses are here. They will be staying overnight with your father."

Kimi and I knew what that meant. My dad would soon pass.

"I wheeled your mom into the living room next to your dad," Olivia said. "They held hands, and your dad said to your mother, 'Are you ready to go to Heaven?' 'Yeah, I'm ready,' your mother said."

Olivia sent Kimi a photo of my parents, my father's hand tightly clasped around my mother's. Her eyes were closed, her face serene. A picture of my parents' deep affection after sixty-eight years of marriage.

That night, my father slept under the effects of morphine.

On Sunday, Sandi, Kimi, and I drove back to see my parents. My father was no longer cognizant, so we chatted with our mother, who was now awake. Occasionally, I would check in on my dad, his eyes shut, his breathing slow, his arms resting at his sides. I felt thankful that he was no longer in pain, but I was saddened by the realization there would be no more time for reminiscing or goodbyes.

As I said goodnight to my mom that evening, she said, "I'm leaving soon."

"You are?"

"Yeah," she said. "And I'm not coming back."

"Are you going to Heaven?"

"Yeah."

I told my mother to hug Sam, her father and my grandpa, for me. She told me she'd give him a hug.

The next morning, the hospice nurse called Kimi's cell phone at 7:30 a.m.

"Your father is unresponsive. He should pass quickly now."

Kimi wanted to rush to my parent's home, a forty-minute drive, but not long after the first call came another. "Your father passed away peacefully," the nurse said. Kimi cried. She hung up the phone. Both of us in tears, we hugged each other tightly. Yet even in this time of grief, I felt blessed. I traveled south because I had thought my mother would be the first to go; instead, I was able to say goodbye to my father. We had one glorious day together while my father was still articulate and animated. An unexpected miracle.

After the phone call, Kimi took me to the airport. I flew home on a plane with only twenty passengers. I didn't need to worry about social distancing after all. Kimi drove back to my parents' home to meet with the funeral home driver who would transport my father to the mortuary. Kimi was with my mother as she kissed her husband's cheek in a final farewell.

My mom didn't leave. The day after my father died, she called Karen.

"I thought I should tell you your grandpa died."

"My mom told me," Karen said.

"Well, I thought you should know so when you come down, you'll know why he won't be here."

We wondered if my mother thought it was her duty to call the family. Did she think Karen was coming to visit? No matter. My mother's call and her gift of sweetness and caring would brighten our day. In our time of sadness, she gave us smiles. Her MO.

Mourning

August 10th. My sixty-seventh birthday. One week after my father's death. Kimi called to wish me a happy birthday, but she had other news, too.

"I saw Mom today. I didn't see her for two days. I can't believe how fast her health has declined. She's eating some, but she has difficulty sitting up in her wheelchair. Sandi and I tried to read some of the cards of condolences sent to Dad, but she didn't seem to hear us. I'm not sure if she'll make it much longer."

"Should I come down?" I said.

"I don't know if you need to. Mom's so frail, and she's not coherent like she was when you were here last week. When I gave her a hug, I asked if she knew who I was. She couldn't speak, but she patted me on the back. Maybe just wait until after she passes."

Kimi was right. I had already said my goodbyes, held the memories close. My sisters would need me more after my mom passed. We had an entire household to go through. My parents had lived in their home for over thirty years. There were photos to sort, files and files of paperwork to go through, family heirlooms to separate out and pass to grandchildren, great-grandchildren. The apprehension about tackling such a huge task made my brain melt like wax.

We were in another heatwave. Temperatures soared into the high nineties, then passed one hundred degrees. We lived at the Sierra snow line. It should not have been this hot. I was exhausted. Fortunately, Lloyd had installed our window air conditioner. Powered by the generator, the fan ran for a few hours in the afternoon. It helped, but life was on hold. I slept, cooked meals, ate, and washed dishes, each day identical to the day before, and each morning I feared looking at my cell phone, afraid that my mother might have died in the night.

Mom died. The dawn was filled with thick smoke. Ash sprinkled our tiny patio, the lawn chairs, our vehicles. The previous evening, lightning had ripped through the night, zapped the earth. Dead leaves, grasses, and branches had burst into flames. We were safe for now, but the massive fires ravaged the lands around us. My stepdaughter and her family had to evacuate from their home. Planes roared overhead. Helicopters whirled. It felt like the entire world was mourning my mother's death.

Kimi called. "We couldn't get Mom's burial date anytime soon. Because of COVID, the funeral home can only do three burials a day. We have to wait two weeks."

"I'll make plane reservations for some time next week. I can help clean out the house before Mom's memorial," I said.

Maybe I sounded confident, but I was a grief-stricken, teeth-grinding wreck. In just a little over two weeks, I had lost both my parents. I wanted to go to my mother's memorial and help my sisters tackle the task of cleaning out our parent's home, but the thought of going back to the claustrophobic city, crowded with people during a pandemic, left me distressed and edgy. Yet, life at home was just as stressful. As wildfires spread across northern California, the weather forecast warned of gusty winds and dry lightning. An acrid whiff of smoke, a plane in the sky, or the sound of a siren off in the distance made my heart pound and my stomach churn.

A few days after Kimi's call, I mustered up enough courage to make plane reservations. Soon, there would be things to do: laundry, packing, shopping. Activities to keep me busy. Untangling my grief, fear, and worry would have to wait.

Burning

As the fires in Northern California continued to burn, I flew south, where I cleaned out my parents' drawers, closets, and cupboards. My sisters and I sifted through important documents, searched through picture albums filled with tiny black-and-white photos. We poured over yellowed scrapbook pages. We tossed outdated papers and duplicate photos, then chose pictures to scan onto a thumb drive: My mother doing the splits on her horse, posing in a handstand on the grass, in a backbend on the sidewalk. Tap-dancing and baton twirling. Always athletic. My mother's sparkle and spirit brought joy to damper our despair.

Karen had driven down during the last few days of my visit. We slow-danced in the living room to my parents' favorite music: the Drifters' "This Magic Moment," The Penguins' "Earth Angel," Johnny Mathis's "Chances Are." We whirled round to doo-wop songs like "Duke of Earl," "There Goes My Baby," "The Lion Sleeps Tonight." Our dancing was bittersweet. Soon, my parents' home would be sold, and our family would no longer gather in these rooms. This would be our last dance.

Later, Karen and I boxed up linens and towels, dishes, silverware, pots, pans, knickknacks, and wall hangings. We hauled numerous bags of trash to large, rented dumpsters. We whittled down my parents' possessions, sorted them into piles of giveaway, sell, or trash. Finally, after my two weeks' stay, Karen and I drove her rental car nine hours back to Northern California. It was a Monday evening, September

7th, when Karen dropped me off in Marysville, where Lloyd picked me up for the hour-plus ride home.

Once home, I wanted to rest and relax, shake off the flurry of the city. I wanted time to reflect and grieve. Instead, life turned more frantic. Tuesday morning, September 8th, the air was stifling hot and slightly smoky, but patches of blue peeked through the gray. I bathed in the forest scents of pine and cedar, then began nesting. I cleaned the bathroom, the refrigerator, and the cupboards, changed the bedding in the screen room. I wrote a grocery list. Made a simple dinner. By evening, the day had cooled, but with it came stronger winds. The Bear Fire was a worry, as there were mandatory evacuations ten miles northeast of our home. Large hot spots burned deep in the rugged canyons to the north. Lloyd and I packed our vehicles just in case, as we were on advisory watch. I kept my phone next to the bed. Checked the fire news each hour, but eventually, I fell asleep.

At 1:00 a.m., I received a short text message from Diane, our neighbor up the hill. "We're under mandatory evacuation orders. Thought you should know."

"Oh, shit." I woke up Lloyd. We stepped into the hazy night. To the south, we could see a bright orange glow, but a southern fire didn't make sense. The Bear Fire had closed all roads to the north, so we would have to travel south towards the fiery light. We threw medications, cell phones, and chargers into our vehicles, turned off the propane tank, closed windows, gathered up the dogs, and locked the trailer. Lloyd led the way in his Dodge truck. I followed in the Jeep. Smoke and dust made visibility poor and driving slow on our backcountry road. Driving became a bit easier once we hit pavement, but as we rounded a sharp bend, an eerie sight came into view. Black trees burned in a blaze of red-orange flames. We heard the fire sizzle, branches crack. A long row of fire engines was parked along the roadside. The pavement was the only clearing as firefighters worked the fire on both sides of the street. They waved us through the nightmare. Sticky with sweat, I tightened my grip on the steering wheel, kept my eyes on Lloyd's taillights until the fire faded behind us.

Fortunately, our ride through the inferno was brief, ten minutes. Still, grief overwhelmed me. I thought of the Paradise fire, two years earlier. I reimagined the horror of the hours-long, slow-trudging ride through the blazing forests my granddaughters had traveled while evacuating their home during the Paradise Camp Fire. A wave of nausea rushed through me.

Around 2:30 in the morning, we arrived at Lloyd's daughter's home. There, we made a bed in the truck for the dogs. Lloyd and I attempted to sleep on the couch, our blankets a tangled mess as we twisted and turned. After that night, we moved from Lloyd's daughter's home to a hotel, then to a friend's home in Nevada, and ended our final evacuation days in Modoc, where we had friends and a clean room at a small motel.

Our evacuation from the fire lasted seven days. We returned home to charred hillsides, blackened trees, and the smell of smoldering ash. We learned later that the fire we had driven through was a new fire, the Willow Fire. It had forced three thousand residents to evacuate and burned 1,311 acres, destroyed forty-one structures.

As the sweltering days dragged on, the Bear Fire to the north had moved closer to our home. The southwest containment lines were out of control; the fire roared up and down the steep canyons, threatening to crest the hills and spread into the small, unincorporated communities below. This included our community. Without electricity, our only available air-conditioning was a small window unit powered by a generator. Its use was limited. Open windows helped cool the trailer at night, but smoke poured inside, stinging my eyes, burning my throat, tightening my chest. I worried about Lloyd, who had COPD and a cough that wouldn't quit.

We couldn't stay. We were technically on evacuation advisory, and we were allowed onto our property with proper identification, but the smoke chased us out. We put our important papers and valuables in storage, repacked our clothing, and headed northeast to Modoc County, the high-country desert where we had lived for fifteen years.

We drove east on Highway 49, a winding forest journey that followed the Yuba River, a road we knew well after living for many years in the Tahoe National Forest. We drove north on Highway 395, an isolated road that followed the Sierra Nevada and eventually crossed the Modoc Plateau through flatlands sprinkled with sagebrush and scrubby juniper pines. After the quiet ride north, we turned east towards the Warner Mountains, where an indigo sky opened wide above us. Incense cedars and aspens dotted the roadside. As we descended into the Great Basin and the tiny town of Cedarville, the world made sense again; colors were in their rightful place, clean air filled my lungs, and the tension I'd been holding for weeks began to subside.

Chapter Ten
Fall 2020

Where Now?

Our trip to Cedarville wasn't just environmentally appealing; reacquainting with old friends gave us a sense of belonging. We ate dinner each night with our dear friends, Ray and Barbara, both authors and editors. We sat on a mix of barstools and old chairs around a wooden bar in the open kitchen/living room, where cast-iron pans hung on the wall and tall Mason jars, filled with rice, oats, and bran, sat on the countertop. We laughed at shared stories, discussed politics and books, ate vanilla ice cream with fresh picked raspberries for dessert. It felt good to bathe in the warmth of friendship.

In the one-street downtown, lined with brick and false-front stores, we ran into other acquaintances. Friends from the farmers market and my old writing group. There were handshakes and hugs. COVID was a minor worry in Cedarville. At the time, Modoc County held steady at just twenty cases.

The high desert also made wildfires less frightening. Like other counties in California, Modoc had its share of fires, typically caused by dry lightning. However, the desert lacked the thick floor of brittle pine needles, densely packed scrub oaks, or the drought-stressed manzanitas that flourished in our foothills. In the Great Basin, one could see a fire coming from miles away.

Lloyd and I wondered if we should look for a new home. Should we return to Modoc, to friends and a more protective geography? It seemed reasonable. We decided to look for homes in Surprise Valley, but in a community of about five hundred people, there weren't many choices. Still, a few houses looked promising. We made three trips to the far eastern corner of California, but each visit led to a dead end.

"Maybe we should broaden our search," Lloyd said. "We need someplace where we feel secure, especially as we age. The summers are just going to get hotter and dryer."

I agreed. Since the Paradise Camp Fire, the smell of smoke, the ominous sound of stirring winds, or a pop and a snap in the trees made the hair rise on my arms. After three fire evacuations, I was tired of the tension, of sleepless nights during red flag warnings and our proximity to raging blazes that lingered for months. I longed for a sense of safety.

We began looking for homes in other rural communities, but the options we found weren't a fit: homes with tiny yards, homes in run-down neighborhoods, homes on pavement with streetlights and sidewalks (heaven forbid).

Eventually, we looked closer to home, higher up our own mountains in the Sierra. There, just thirty minutes from our property, we found a cabin in an unincorporated community of under two hundred people. The landscape was different than our ten acres. It was higher elevation, 3,550 feet versus 2400 hundred feet. It would be cooler—a plus for me. And the community was certified as fire-wise safe, meaning the forest floor had been thinned of vegetation, such as small trees, shrubs, and ground cover that could fuel fires. The tall, healthy pines stood strong and green. We would still be in high-fire-risk country, but the cabin was surrounded by defensible space. There was electricity, a local water source, a fire hydrant near the house, a fire department down the street. We made an offer on the cabin, and in just a few weeks, we were in escrow.

Lloyd and I still wanted to keep the trailer and ten acres for recreation, but we didn't want to continue to drop large sums of money into a place that could burn, and we couldn't insure. Living in a trailer off a long dirt road, where escaping a fast-moving fire would be difficult, spooked us. Still, we loved the land, and using it as an isolated retreat was appealing. An insured home with luxuries like fire hydrants, lights, and an actual address seemed like a good place to settle.

Why So Worried?

We wanted to prepare for our move, but first, we had to make the trailer winter ready. Lloyd and I had a sixty-day escrow and would not be able to move into our new cabin until the end of December. At the trailer, Lloyd installed extra batteries for our dimming solar lights, as the shortened days meant less sun on the solar panels. The batteries would store power for the darker hours. I got out our camp lanterns and inserted new batteries into each lamp. The lamps would provide evening light and allow us to save our solar lights for tasks like cooking, washing dishes, and other chores that required bright light.

Lloyd hooked up our Mr. Heater, a propane model that could provide instant heat when building a fire in the woodstove wasn't convenient. Because the woodstove was our main heat source, we cut and stacked piles of wood. With the slew of fallen branches from the powerful autumn winds, wood was plentiful. Gathering the downed limbs would also help clear the forest floor.

Together, Lloyd and I stapled tarps on the walls of the screened-in bedroom to protect it from rain. We packed up the shade canopy that we no longer needed. Lloyd and I found our rhythm. We enjoyed the physical activity, alternating the hard work with breaks and naps. Moments sitting in the sun or after dinner reading brought a bit of peace, but like most people during this time of wildfires and a pandemic, we felt jittery. Uncertain. Was it safe to visit our kids and grandchildren? What about the upcoming holidays? Should we return to our self-imposed lockdown? As Thanksgiving approached, coronavirus cases surged in our communities.

I worried about the timing of our move. Could we get into the house to quarantine safely if necessary? A place where we could have a hot shower, more room to spread out if isolation was required? As Lloyd and I journeyed through fall and into winter, my mind often returned to the words of a Merle Haggard song:

If we make it through December
Everything' s gonna be all right, I know
It's the coldest time of winter
And I shiver when I see the falling snow.

Haggard' s narrator was a factory worker, laid off just before Christmas. Lloyd and I felt fortunate to be retired. We hadn't lost jobs like others did during the pandemic. We didn't have a large income, but we made enough for our simple lifestyle. Still, with daily news headlines like, "We Are Entering COVID Hell," or "Beware COVID-19's Third Wave," it was hard to shrug off the nagging feeling of foreboding.

Counting Down the Days

The rains came. The first deluge lasted just three days, but the downpours were enough to soak the earth and pack the dust. High humidity and cold mornings soon followed, so even though sunny days returned, we were allowed to burn. Lloyd spent days clipping back brush; he thinned tiny pines and burned last year's brush piles that lay dry and crunchy. It felt good to sit by the fire or rake branches into a neat circle. For years, I had built and tended campfires in the backcountry and burned piles on our properties, took care of sacred fires for a sweat lodge. Watching the flickering flames had a hypnotic effect. Fire could instill both fear and calm. Those days of fall burnings were peaceful.

There was still enough sunlight for a load of laundry to dry on the clothesline. The extra days of sunshine allowed me to avoid the laundromat and a drive to town. The shortened days, however, left little sunlight on our solar panels. Even with extra batteries, there was never enough light for cooking or reading at night. Lloyd loved the soft light of kerosene lamps, but with two dogs and two adults in a three-hundred-square-foot space, we risked knocking over a lamp. We brought out the battery lamps. They helped some but cooking in the kitchen was rough. I used a large flashlight to check whatever was cooking in the oven. The lack of bright light led to discussions of what we were eating. I'd explain the table layout to Lloyd.

"There's leftover turkey and stuffing with gravy on your plate," I'd say. "I didn't have leftover potatoes, so we've got asparagus. I made a salad. It's in the bowl next to the lamp."

Without our outdoor solar shower, we took bucket baths in the bathtub. Short on the numerous solar panels required to ignite the new on-demand water heater Lloyd had installed, we gave up. Instead, we waited for the arrival of a propane camp shower or our move to the new house. We didn't know which would come first. In the meantime, I sat on a shower stool and poured stove-heated water from a large pot over my long, graying hair. This became a mid-morning task, as the evening was too dark and damp. Once I had myself soaped, washed, and rinsed, I sat outside while the sun dried my hair. As romantic as that may sound, I was counting down the days until we could move into our cabin and take a real shower.

I wish I could say I was no longer anxious, but COVID was raging across the state, and hospital capacity was diminishing. Our community was a part of two small counties that shared one hospital. The ICU and ER beds were already full, and like other small communities, staffing was a problem. The traveling nurses who typically filled in the gaps were in short supply.

Three more weeks. That was the amount of time until our planned move-in date. At one point during those weeks, Lloyd had a sore throat, chills, and body aches. He was tested for COVID, then we frantically waited for his results for two days. Negative. We were grateful, but still, "it" was out there.

We now had close family and friends who had been affected by the pandemic. I felt that if we could just move into our cabin, I'd be okay. At least if I got COVID, I would have my own room and bathroom to keep the infection away from Lloyd. I could take a steamy bath in pink Himalayan salts. Put laundry in a hot dryer. Isolate at home in luxury. My off-grid, hippie bliss was dissolving. I still needed forests and space, but in these difficult times, a bit of conventional comfort wouldn't hurt.

Stay at Home

Near the end of 2020, the word *turmoil* seemed to describe life for many people throughout the world. Fires and heat continued to ravage the planet, and COVID-19 kept surging. By mid-December, stay-at-home orders were revived. Hospitalizations and deaths reached new heights daily. A vaccine was on its way, but it would take many months to tame the monster. Emergency stay-at-home warnings flashed on my cell phone, and while I was grocery shopping one day, alarms blared the alert. The store was closing due to the increasing positivity rates in the area.

Layered alongside my vigilance against the virus was the un-certainty of where we would live. Our move-in date kept changing, drifting further away. I felt directionless. Unable to find footing. Lloyd and I still had clothing and furnishings in storage. I had filled the screen room with items to take to the new house. Boxes of towels, sheets, blankets, sweaters, and boots were taped and labeled. Plastic tubs held dishes, pots, and pans. I'd often go to my closet to get a shirt or a sweater, only to remember it was packed. Our clothing and furnishings were too spread out. I wasn't sure what to do. Unpack? Wait it out? For how long?

After a long delay, we eventually heard from our realtor, Steve, about a closing date. The seller had agreed to a date one week later than initially planned. Steve told us, "She's not feeling well and moving a bit slow. Her original plans to live in a tiny house fell through, and she hasn't found another place to live yet, but she thinks she can be out on time."

She thinks?!

Another week went by, then another call from Steve. "I just wanted you to know that the seller has found a place to live. She'll be moving out this weekend."

I melted with relief. We had a direction, a plan. I liked plans. Lloyd and I could finally sort out our belongings that were still in storage. I could get organized, and I loved organization. Due to my untidy and often cluttered mind, having an organized home was a priority, and it gave me a sense of peace. I could stay at home and nest in the cabin. And we still had our land. Grateful for the abundance, I thanked the heavens, the stars, the ancestors, and the creator.

Chapter Eleven
Winter 2020

Christmas Wishes

Wind howled outside the windows. Rain drummed on the roof. I watched as leaves scattered across the yard and branches fell from trees. Christmas Day. I indulged myself, dropped a dollop of whipped cream into my coffee. The cup warmed my hands as I drank in small sips. A fire burned in the woodstove; the air smelled of smoke. Lloyd and I spent the day making calls to our families, reading, and napping. We ate an early dinner, had pie for dessert. Starburst battery lights hung from the windows, giving the room a bit of sparkle.

I missed my parents. My dad loved Christmas. Our family traveled south for holiday visits when my kids were growing up, and my dad spent months preparing for his Christmas games. This tradition began with my grandmother, my father's mom, who always had a grab bag of presents where one could pick out a simple surprise gift. My father's version of the grab bag grew to greater proportions. Each year, he'd include all types of gifts, from socks, duct tape, and tool sets, to bicycles, electronics, and cash.

He'd change the games each year. The grab bag became an exchange game, where one could trade gifts using the more elaborate gifts as "trading power." His cash gifts were incorporated into a money tree, where each family member could pick an envelope. The amounts ranged from twenty to one-hundred-dollar bills. Later, he added a spin-the-wheel game. Wherever your number landed, there was a present to match the number. It seemed like every year my father became more génèrons—more expensive gifts were added, larger amounts of cash.

After my father passed away, and my sisters and I were cleaning out his file cabinets, we found notebooks filled with my father's neat hand-printing. He had written out the rules for each of his Christmas games. He had even included diagrams.

Thinking about my father's games made me smile, yet the contrast between those loud, boisterous Christmas pasts at my parents' home and our now quiet seclusion due to COVID made Christmas 2020 a bit melancholy. Like so many others that winter, we were separated from our families; we longed to see the excited, smiling faces of our grandchildren as they opened gifts. We, the senior citizens at the time, didn't want to spend our holidays alone, but we were encouraged to stay home. Stay safe. And so, we did.

I was wearing down, but hopeful that our move into our new home might make life better.

A few days after Christmas, just before our planned move, Steve called. "We have another problem with the house sale. The underwriter noticed that one of the home inspectors stated that the decks' undersides were covered in mold and had to be torn down and replaced. The seller wants another contractor to look at it, hoping for a different outcome."

The seller had already moved out to a rental home, but when the results from the new contractor/inspector came back with the same conclusion, the seller backed out. She didn't want to put any money into building, and she couldn't sell it in its current condition. After more than two months of waiting, Lloyd and I lost the house.

We tried to find another place, but with so few homes on the market, buyers were making offers sight unseen. By the time we could get an appointment to view a home, a sale would be pending. The act of hunting for a house was both delightful and stressful. Imagining ourselves in a new place with real lighting and a larger space, planning how our furnishings would fit into each room, and gazing online at comfy recliners or brightly colored Native American rugs brought hope. Then suddenly, the dream would dissolve as houses were snatched up by other buyers. With so many emotional difficulties, I'd often slip into a chronic fatigue crash, and the daybed in the trailer's main living area became the center of my life. I couldn't tolerate sensory stimuli: noise or light sent me cringing. For days, I would stop reading and writing. My daily walks down the meadow road were rare.

Some days, I had to drive to town to do laundry. Our washing machine needed replacement parts, and it was too cold to line-dry clothes. I drove to town early to avoid crowds. I avoided people by tossing my laundry into the washing machines, then returning to the quiet of my Jeep. Checking the time, twenty-four minutes later, I removed the wet clothes from the machines, dumped them into a rolling basket, stuffed them into the dryer, then rushed back to the Jeep. After another twenty-four minutes, I took the laundry out of the dryer. I tried to fold the clothes on the large white laundry table, but a television mounted on the wall competed with loud ' 80s music on the attendant's computer. I couldn't tolerate the noise. I covered my ears with my hands, gathered up four loads of warm laundry, and threw them into the back of my vehicle.

I was desperate to escape the hectic scene of the city. I needed to stop for gas, but I couldn't bear the thought of a television blaring at the gas pump. Was there anywhere in a small city without noise? I' d get gas later in our home community, as the gas pumps there were old-fashioned. No televisions at the pumps to stimulate panic. As soon as I drove off the pavement and onto our dirt road, my pulse and breathing slowed.

Chapter Twelve
Winter 2021

Fugacious Dreams

By the end of January 2021, Lloyd and I had hunted for houses from the northern California and Oregon border all the way south to Placer County. Often, we'd find something we loved: a level, forested, and fenced acreage beneath snow-covered mountains; a large, fully fenced parcel with healthy pines, firs, and cedars, a place where dogs could run. We saw homes with rustic charm: walls of cream-color adobe or hand-hewn logs, lava rock fireplaces, hardwood floors, large windows, and archways.

We made offers; occasionally, we were the highest bidders, but sellers seemed to be turned off by our VA loan. When excitement stirred over a new possibility, I'd send pictures to Karen, but when home after home fell through, she texted, "Maybe take a break from looking for a while. I'm emotionally invested, too, and it's really hard." I knew what she meant. I had loved one cabin so much that, when we lost it, I felt like I had lost a lover.

Snow, high winds, and gray skies. Lloyd and I woke early to view another house. Fortunately, it was only about twenty minutes from our property, but we would need extra driving time, as the nights' wind would cause branches to crack and fall across our muddy road. Lloyd carried a saw in his truck. During the winter, it was often used.

The truck splashed through deep pools of water and slogged through mud, but once we hit pavement, the road was clear. The creek running along the roadside was a frothy swirl. Snow quickly turned to hard rain as we drove down the hill, where the geography changed to jade-green grasses and a panoramic view of the valley below. We turned off the pavement and onto a gravel road. Without mud holes or ruts, the drive was easy.

The home was a modular. Nothing special. It needed paint. The toilet bowls were black with filth. A broken window in the bathroom. Mildew in the laundry room. Yet, the five acres where the house stood were pleasing. Thick-branched Heritage Oaks rose stately in the yard. Kale, chard, and cabbage flourished in an untended garden. A stream flowed through the back of the property. Still, the fixer-upper was priced higher than our failed offer on my dream cabin on forested acreage near Mount Lassen.

While talking to Steve about making a potential offer, he told us, "The realtor selling the home told me that he already had two generous offers."

Say what? The house was just listed. Steve then revealed that the two offers were "in-house." We made an offer without enthusiasm or expectations.

Later that evening, after our offer was signed and delivered, Lloyd called Steve. "Can you pull the offer we made on the house this morning?"

Lloyd and I had decided not to settle. Buying a home that was priced too high and needed work just to make it livable was not an option. We would wait until we found a move-in-ready home. Steve canceled the documents.

We later learned that realtors were snatching up homes in our price range. Their flipping houses left buyers like us out of the market. Lloyd and I had bought many homes over the years, and we had yet to see times like these. No wonder so many working people were home-insecure or homeless. It felt hopeless. Not just for us, but for others, like my children and the numerous Paradise Camp Fire survivors who still lived in FEMA trailers or tents in the Chico parks. How would they find permanent homes with prices so high?

February 2021. The tiny daffodils scattered around the trailer began their opening; petals unfurled to show bright orange trumpets. For a moment, a hint of spring, of new beginnings, but by evening, the winds came, and another storm blew in. That night, cooking in the darkened kitchen, I was attempting to open a can of black beans when the ring on the pull tab broke. I tried to use a can opener, but it didn't fit the size of the can. I pounded the lid with a knife, denting the can. Finally, I clenched the hair on my head with both fists, cried, "It's so hard."

Lloyd heard me and said, "Yes, it is." He brought over his sharpest knife and opened the can.

Somehow, hearing Lloyd confirm my feelings provided some relief. Life *was* hard. Both of Lloyd's chainsaws broke down on the same day. He had to order parts, so he couldn't cut wood. Later, the rains became an atmospheric river pouring from the sky. Strong winds made outdoors a danger. We were out of propane for our Mr. Heater, and I tried to buy small camp propane canisters for my smaller propane heater and Enviro-Logs for the woodstove, but the store was sold out. We needed more batteries for the camp lights. More gas for the generator. We were behind on our big-town shopping due to other appointments: Lloyd's out-of-town dental, doctor, and eye care visits; my trips to the pharmacy and to our local medical clinic for my monthly B12 injections. Searching for homes added more time commitments and stress.

Once the storm cleared, we jumped into our big Dodge truck, bought propane, gas, and batteries. Lloyd found the parts to fix his chainsaws. He cut more wood. The days grew longer. Soon, there would be light when I cooked dinner.

I walked the dogs down the wet meadow trail. Mosses covered oaks and stones in velvety greens. Puddles had become pools; streams of water rushed across the road. A covey of quail flew up out of the leaves, startled by the dogs. I felt gratitude for the opportunity to live in such a place, but I knew this home was temporal. My mind wandered: I thought about George and Lennie from Steinbeck's *Of Mice and Men*. Of Lennie's dream to buy a little farmhouse with lots of rabbits, a place they could grow their own food. I wondered if Lloyd and I would eventually find a home, or if the search was merely a fugacious dream.

Are We There Yet?

After months of uncertainty, we made an offer on a little white house on four and a half acres. The seller accepted the offer.

The 1,075-square-foot house wasn't our first choice. It was too close to the road. In 1945, when the house was built, the road access would have been an advantage on snowy winter days. We feared traffic, but this was not a big concern in a community of three hundred people. The paved road ended in gravel and dirt. And besides, the place had charm. A large screened-in porch ran along the entire front of the house. The slate-gray tin roof was shiny and new. Inside, the dual-pane windows were large and bright. Light gleamed on knotty pine walls. The acreage was forested, but cleaned and de-brushed.

Ironically, Karen had sent me the web page for this house when we first began looking, but we didn't think the home would pass the VA loan requirements. Too old. We looked elsewhere, but after switching to a conventional loan, we returned. Seeing the home again with the realtor opened our eyes to its appeal: polished floors, an open living/ dining area with a woodstove, new paint outside, real wood cabinets in the kitchen, two bonus rooms upstairs, and an air conditioner and heating unit. The place was turnkey, and I didn't want another fixer upper. I was burned out on cleaning, painting, and remodeling other people' s neglected properties. For me, the home' s tidiness was its biggest asset.

Usually, I didn't mind paperwork, but buying a home with all the documents online was difficult. I had only the iPhone. The tiny lettering on the forms was almost impossible to read, and without electricity, Lloyd and I didn't have the consistency of Wi-Fi. Our Internet connection was intermittent and so slow that I would sometimes wait forty-five minutes for a document to load. Then, when I was trying to complete the signing process, my phone would go dead. Several times, I made the forty-five-minute drive to town to meet with our loan officer to make copies or complete a computer task I was unable to perform on the iPhone. Worrying that another buyer might swoop in and steal our offer while I slowly plodded through escrow documents had my insides tangled in knots.

When we finally completed the home inspections, sent in a plethora of financial disclosures, reviewed, and signed the seller' s disclosures, and provided proof of homeowner insurance, we hit another hurdle. We couldn't get an appointment with an appraiser. Two weeks went by after my check to the appraisal company had cleared; still no date. Tossed into another unknown, I feared we' d miss our window of opportunity, and I didn't have the wherewithal to make it through a third round of escrow. Even if we had an appraisal date, I feared the appraiser might determine that the home had a lower market value than the sales price. The lender could reject the mortgage. I tried to "go with the flow," but all I could visualize were my experiences rafting the American River: three- to four-foot waves and drops and maneuvering through narrow passages, large rocks, and turbulent rapids.

Yet, some days saw calm waters. Mid-February 2021 looked and felt like spring. Daffodils popped up over the hillsides. Crocuses bloomed in purples and blues. Weather remained in the high sixties and low seventies. I took advantage of the good weather on weekends, bringing my granddaughters to the park. Annie loved this outdoor time and having the space to run. She ran in circles around the park borders, making her own track. Marie spent her time collecting dead camellias that had fallen off their colorful bushes and onto the ground. She'd make flower arrangements on the park bench: a circle of brownish-pink flowers surrounding a plastic Coke bottle with a reddish-brown camellia on top; a blend of red and pink camellias piled inside my upside-down hat. Later, Marie would offer flowers to other children. When it was time to leave the park, she would place the remaining flowers in a bag to take home. There, she would add yellow dandelions and green clover to the mix.

The good days were a soothing tonic and a distraction from other bumps in the road. Lloyd had started having seizures weekly. The seizures had begun three years prior, but they were intermittent. Back then, the VA had sent Lloyd to a hospital for an EEG, but there was no sign of epilepsy, so they mailed Lloyd medication and made bimonthly phone appointments with a neurologist. Near the end of February, Lloyd saw a new neurologist who read his file. Alarmed, she immediately made a call to San Francisco's VA Hospital. After several talks with the specialists there, Lloyd was scheduled for inpatient testing. He would be in the hospital three to seven days. Or longer, depending on the outcome. Lloyd and I tried not to focus on the what ifs. It was too overwhelming. Our major concern was moving into a house that could offer a bit more safety. Having a home with an address, on a road that medical personnel could find, would lower my worry rate. Paved access and a level lot suddenly seemed appealing.

On day thirty of our escrow, we waited anxiously for the appraisal report to arrive. We had heard of other buyers losing homes due to inflated prices. If the appraisal came in low, we would have to make up the difference.

"I know the house won't be appraised for the selling price," Lloyd said. "We will need to decide how much of a difference we can pay."

I got out a calculator and made-up various prices the appraiser might come up with. A depressing endeavor. At the low estimates I gave the house, we could never afford to buy. I felt defeated, and the not-knowing made my throat tighten. We waited until noon, then Lloyd called our realtor.

"Steve said the appraiser will complete the documents within the hour. He didn't want to call until he had the information," Lloyd told me.

Two hours later, Lloyd received an email with the sixty-page document that could only be downloaded with Adobe. Neither Lloyd nor I had Adobe on our phones. It took some time, but I eventually found a free Adobe application. Once we had the pages opened, we could barely read the minute print, and we couldn't find the appraised amount hidden in the copious text. At this point, we were desperate. Lloyd called Steve, who told us the amount. It mirrored the seller's asking price. Lloyd and I released long, audible sighs. Emotionally exhausted, we staggered to the bedroom for a nap.

Chapter Thirteen
Spring 2021

Friends in High Places

By mid-spring, summer blazed. Unseasonal heat and strong winds led to red flag warnings. Already, the land had cracked and dried. Reservoirs had shrunk to inconceivable low levels, but there was a bright side. People were outdoors. COVID numbers had dropped. Lloyd and I, emboldened by our COVID vaccines, started mingling with humans again.

Even though we were now living full time in our new home, we tried to maintain relationships with our small community on the hill. On trailer days, I frequently visited with Diane. She was the "mom" of the hill, often cooking meals for her neighbors. She rode down from her RV homestead on the hill-top on her quad, gifting us with honey from her hives, flowers, or home-made cookies.

Diane and her closest neighbor, Jerry, were instrumental in keeping us connected to the hill-top dwellers. Because most of the dirt roads on the hill were gated, one needed combination numbers for the locks, or another way in. Jerry had both. His property was above ours. Jerry would pick us up in his side by side, a 4 X 4 utility vehicle with a bench seat. We'd squish into the seat, then ride the trails while manzanita and brush slapped Lloyd in the face. I took the middle seat, avoiding the thrashing. Diane traveled in front of us on her own ATV. The four of us rode though "Jerry's Trails," stopping to look at glorious views of the lake below, a hidden artesian well, or to visit with the boys.

Of course, the boys weren't really that young— their ages ranged from the late twenties to early forties. Brad, his wild, curly hair often pulled up in a top knot, owned a lot of acreage and a thriving business. He lived in a lovely older cabin, fully decked out in solar. His land was lush with trees. Several greenhouses sat in neat rows. Nearby, a picnic table, flowers, and veggies in raised beds added to the tidy charm. A couple of Brad's workers lived in smaller, less elaborate cabins or trailers. Higher up the hill, a young couple owned a trailer with a large, stick-built addition. Their covered back porch overlooked the lake. A perfect spot for morning coffee or a cold beer on a hot day.

It's difficult to explain the connection I felt towards my neighbors. Except for Diane and Jerry, who were in our age range, we didn't visit the hill-top often. But we shared a sense of community some might call unconventional: self-sufficient, off road and off grid.

Our shared lifestyles included elements others might not prioritize. Certain tools were vital—chainsaws, handsaws, axes, and battery drills were at the ready in every vehicle. Generators were mandatory. Without them, we couldn't pump our wells. With the ongoing drought, talk often included the current GPM (gallons pumped per minute) or a tank's water level. We all had various forms of solar, from elaborate with numerous panels, to simply one panel and a few batteries like Lloyd and I had. We discussed gardening vegetables, flowers, and medicinal plants: soils, compost, water, lighting systems, seeds, clones, and growing cycles. For Lloyd and me, long time participants in the back-to-the-land movement, it was refreshing to see a younger generation dedicated to simple, green living.

Best Day Ever

June 12th, 2021. Marie's eighth birthday. We were having a party in Bille Park in Paradise. It had recently opened in April after the removal of over five hundred hazardous trees and the rebuilding of burnt structures. The rugged trails on the canyon had closed, but the center of the park was open. The still-standing trees offered shade, and the large, open lawn, though no longer lush and green, provided plenty of running space for the girls.

The picnic table was draped in a pink tablecloth. Cake, pizza, watermelon, and presents were piled on top. More presents sat next to the table. I brought a rainbow-colored piñata, and it hung off a tree branch. I also brought a corn toss game and bubbles.

Marie was excited. Her long, blonde hair was pulled into a pony-tail; a glittery, red "Birthday Girl" Tierra crowned her head. A smile lit her face. Looking older than her eleven years, Annie's hair hung loose. She wore a tie-dyed tank top. The girls took swings at the piñata, hitting it hard until it finally broke open and candy and small toys fell to the ground where they were greedily grabbed and stuffed into pockets. We sang "Happy Birthday" as Marie blew out candles.

Afterwards, she opened her presents. Later, as Marie's party ended, she hugged me tight and said, "This was the best day ever."

My drive home was bittersweet—filled with the joy of family, yet sad, as Annie and Marie would return "home" to a crowded hotel room. Several weeks earlier, my granddaughters' mother had received a letter stating her family needed to vacate the FEMA camp. I had no idea how FEMA chose who would be the first to go, but my granddaughters were in that group. Their stepdad had bought a modular home near Paradise, but it hadn't been completed. It didn't' matter. They were forced to leave. Once again, their family had moved into a hotel room. I couldn't bear the thought of my granddaughters living in that cramped space. The landscape around me felt bleak. Instead of tall pines and majestic oaks, blackened trees remained. Dry, untamed grasses grew on leveled lots where houses once stood. On cleared lots, an occasional new modular home sat on bare, red earth. And yet. As I drove the winding road towards home, huge valley views opened before me. Without trees, I could see for miles. Shallow rice ponds reflected swaths of silver. Soft squares of gold and green fields lay below undulating hills dotted with oaks. I could hear Marie's voice: "Best day ever."

Chapter Fourteen
Summer 2021

The Black Crow

Mid-July 2021. I called Karen in the morning. She sounded distressed.

"I've been watching three baby birds in their tree-nest for several days, but this morning, a black crow swooped down and snatched one of the birds and flew off with it in its beak. When I went to check the nest, I found two tiny birds in the grass," Karen said.

She had contacted a nature center to find out if she should put the birds back in the nest. The expert told Karen that, because the babies were so young, they could be returned.

"But what if the crow comes back?" Karen said.

"We'll have to let nature take its course," was the expert's response.

"Not on my watch," Karen said, but not out loud.

Like me, Karen was an empath—we feel the emotions and energy of others deeply, and our love for animals is equal to humans. Karen *had* to save the birds. She covered her hands with socks and gently lifted the babies into their nest. She had kept watch throughout the day, just in case the crow reappeared. Eventually, mommy and daddy bird flew home to take care of their offspring.

Earlier that week, our small home had filled with company—Lloyd's younger brother, John, and his wife, Grace, had driven down from Oregon. Our dogs, Jackson and Little Bit, had company, too: the gentle, wrinkled-faced Bulldog, Leo. Jackson and Leo were older dogs. At twelve and eleven, they were content to lounge on the front porch. Little Bit was four, still wild and bustling with energy. As the alpha female, she bossed the bigger dogs, stealing their treats and pushing in for first dibs at dinner. Her exuberance soared throughout the house as she jumped over the couch or ran up and down the stairs. Outside, in her one-acre fenced yard, Little Bit was rambunctious, chasing squirrels or lizards. She was fearless and unafraid of the coyotes that roamed and howled nearby. Even the black bears who walked along our fence line didn't faze her.

A typical husky, she was a runner and an escape artist. Those traits I could manage when Lloyd and I lived on our other property, far away from paved roads. Her inability to heed the command *come* wasn't an issue there. Occasionally, however, I worried I wouldn't be able to keep her safe. After Lloyd and I bought our current house, he immediately built a strong, secure fence. Still, several times over the first few months in our new home, Little Bit had slipped out onto the road—when a friend left a gate open, when she jumped onto downed logs then climbed over the fence, when she hopped out of the Jeep before I could attach her leash to her collar. Each time, any attempt to go after her was fruitless. She only ran further away. We had learned to stand guard—watch her wander the woods across the road, praying a car wouldn't come by until she made up her mind to come home through the gate we had left open for her. This method of letting her return home on her own terms worked but left me a fretful wreck.

For the first several months in our new home, Little Bit managed to avoid the dangers of the street. Until the day the crow snatched the bird. The same day company distracted us, as more of Lloyd's relatives had come to visit that afternoon. Later, as our guests were leaving, the gate opened as the group headed towards their SUV. Little Bit, the cunning opportunist, slipped out, too. I saw her run across the road and into the thick woods. She was safe there, but she wouldn't stay put. She was busy—chasing lizards, digging in the dirt, zigzagging across the road. She wouldn't come when I called. I needed to get her leashed, but she wasn't having it. The few cars on the road slowed when they saw her. Except the shiny, red car.

The one that flew down the road at racing speed. I screamed when I heard the thump. The car swerved, but the driver never stopped. *Bastard!* Lloyd ran into the street, swooped up Little Bit, who laid limp in his arms.

Lloyd placed Little Bit on a soft blanket on a table in the back yard. I stood over her, wailing, snot running down my nose. I reached over and hugged her. Stroked her fine fur. She was warm. Perfect. No blood, no apparent broken bones. But she wasn't breathing. I stayed with Little Bit, sobbing, sobbing, sobbing, while Lloyd and his brother, John, dug her grave.

I spoke to her, "Thank you, Little Bit, for helping me heal. For bringing life to my wild side, for running uninhibited when I could no longer run. For your feral nature…" I kept talking—my words incoherent. I couldn't stop. If I did, she'd be gone.

When Lloyd and John finished digging, Lloyd put sweet smelling cedar branches over the earth. He wrapped Little Bit in her favorite blanket, placed her on the cedar bed. Grace came out, and we took turns telling Little Bit how much she was loved. After we spoke, we each sprinkled her with sweet sage and incense cedar. John and Lloyd shoveled the mound of earth over my beloved dog. Grace had picked wildflowers, placed them on the mound. When the others returned to the house, I sat with Little Bit. I couldn't move with my heart in so many pieces. Towards twilight, I rose and walked away. Once inside the house, I took an Aleve PM, staggered into bed, and waited for numbness to quiet the anguish.

Saint Martin

Without Little Bit, there was too much space in the house. Too much quiet. Jackson seemed lost. Or maybe that was me. I wept for my sweet, little dog, wanted to hold her memory, but I needed more. I needed a puppy.

I was terrified of telling my granddaughters about Little Bit's death. Especially Annie, who was smitten by Little Bit's charm. I knew there'd be tears. Too much loss. We needed a gain. I waited just one week after Little Bit died, then searched the internet for the closest pet rescue agencies until I found a possible pup. I filled out the adoption forms, but because adoptions were first come, first served, there was no guarantee I'd get the dog I had chosen. I called Annie.

"I have some sad news. Little Bit was hit by a car, and she died." I paused, let Annie gulp in her sobs. "She wasn't in any pain. We buried her in the backyard. I'm sorry, Annie."

I let Annie recover a bit. "I'm going to adopt a puppy. Do you want to come with me to help pick it out? Karen's coming, too. We can choose a new dog together."

"I' ve never adopted a dog before. I would like that," Annie said.

We planned our trip to the pet rescue the following weekend. I picked up Annie at Jake' s trailer. Karen met us at the rescue center. When we walked inside, Annie was overjoyed.

"I' ve never seen so many puppies. How will we choose just one?" she said.

The female pup I had picked out was already gone, as female dogs were adopted quickly. We walked around the center. Some puppies were in a large play area, others were in their crates. While some dogs were calm, others yelped and howled. One old dog growled like a demon. Her fur—a shaggy mess. She had round, dark eyes and a sinister snarl. *Who would adopt her?* I felt a bit sad for the grouchy old bitch.

"I want a puppy, so we' ll look at those first. We also want a dog that' s not nervous around people," I said.

Annie, Karen, and I walked through the building, petting the dogs, delighting in their animal vibe. Annie picked out a young pup. He was adorable—a tiny ball of soft, silky, chocolate fur.

"Can we look at this one?" Annie said. She knew we could ask the volunteers to open the crate and take the dog to an outdoor play area.

"Let' s look at a few more. Then we can see how they do outside."

Looking around, I found a corner we had missed. On the crate tag, was the name of the dog I had wanted, Crete Red, but inside, there was a male dog, Saint Martin. At three-months-old, he looked just like the photo I' d seen of his sister—white coat with light-tan spots, large brown eyes, and floppy ears. He was calm and gently licked Annie' s fingers through the crate. Saint Martin was a Yellow Labrador Retriever / Dachshund mix.

"I like him," Annie said. "Can we take him out, too?"

We took the tiny chocolate pup to the outdoor area first. Annie, Karen, and I sat inside a circled dog fence. Annie placed the pup in her lap.

"He's shaking," she said. The poor thing was frightened. He was too young, not ready to leave his mama, but that' s probably why he was in a rescue center.

"Let's look at Saint Martin," I said.

A volunteer came out to take the puppy back to his cage. She returned with Saint Martin in her arms, then placed him inside the circle. Saint Martin cuddled next to Annie, licked her fingers. He wasn' t shaky or nervous. He had a calm demeanor, and he oozed with sweetness.

"I like this one," Annie said.

Saint Martin scampered over to Karen and me. We were both instantly charmed. "I think he' s the one," I said. Annie eagerly agreed.

While I finished filling out paperwork and Saint Martin got his final shot, Annie looked at the paperwork and said, "Wow. Adopting a dog is a lot of work. It' s like homework." I smiled at the thought.

After I brought Saint Martin home, he proved to be all that we wanted—good natured, easy to potty-train, intelligent, and an excellent cuddle buddy for Annie, and of course me. The only thing I wanted to change was his name. Annie and I tried other names, but they didn' t stick. Karen sent an email. "I found this information about Saint Martin. I think his name is perfect."

St. Martin de Porres was born in Lima, Peru, on December 9, 1579. Martin was the illegitimate son to a Spanish gentleman and a freed slave from Panama, of African or possibly Native American descent. At a young age, Martin's father abandoned him, his mother, and his younger sister, leaving Martin to grow up in deep poverty. As Martin grew older, he experienced a great deal of ridicule for being of mixed-race. Martin's life reflected his great love for God and all of God's gifts. It is said he had many extraordinary abilities, including miraculous knowledge, spiritual knowledge, and an excellent relationship with animals. Martin also founded an orphanage for abandoned children and slaves and is known for raising dowry for young girls in short amounts of time. (catholic.org)

St. Martin later became the patron saint of people of mixed race. We decided to keep the name, calling our new dog Martin in honor of such a kind and generous man.

Fire–Again

I had been reading the news regularly, concerned about the large Dixie Fire that began on July 27th in the town of Belden. While Belden was not much of a town, with a population of around twenty-two people, it was a place I knew well. I had camped there when my children were young. Later, it would become a stopping point for refreshments after day hiking the Ben Lomond, Indian Creek, or Yellow Creek trails.

Because Belden was just twenty-three miles from Pulga, the location where the Paradise Camp Fire began, I checked in on the Dixie Fire daily. On a hot, smoky Wednesday, while scanning the news, I saw that a new fire had started, and it was close to home.

> "August 11, 2021, at 3:31 PM. Vegetation fire. Air Attack is reporting the fire is burning at a moderate to dangerous rate of spread. Requesting additional helicopters and tankers. Evacuations are being initiated." (YubaNet)

As I read the news, I felt sick. *Shit. Not again.* I was mourning the one-year anniversary of my parents' passing, and it seemed impossible to summon up the energy to pack for an evacuation. Looking at the fire map, I saw that our off-grid trailer and ten acres were near the dirt road where the fire had sparked and spread. But the winds were spiraling northeast, towards our new home. Would the trailer be spared? Or would the winds push further north, threatening our house?

I had no time to ponder these questions. We were soon on evacuation advisory. Lloyd and I immediately went into our packing routine. I placed the tub filled with important documents in the back of the Jeep along with clothes, medications, laptops, and chargers. I filled a bag with necessities for our dogs—food, treats, water, bowls, toys, and leashes. My Jeep was already supplied with quick-escape essentials: first aid supplies, towels, flashlights, camp lanterns, hygiene items, a fire extinguisher, and my faithful Leatherman multi-knife and tool set. Lloyd packed up the Dodge truck with his clothes, tools, and family heirlooms.

On a physical level, my movements controlled, I knew what had to be done. My mind, on the other hand, was a chaotic mess, cluttered with what ifs, scattered thoughts, and worry. I was jumpy and jittery.

As we waited anxiously for more news, we made plans. I looked on the Internet for hotels to the north in Butte County, but most hotels were full. Besides, the prices were outrageous: $250 for one night. No way. Lloyd's daughters both called and offered their homes in the Grass Valley area. Having housing options provided a bit of peace, so we waited it out. The evacuation order was now one mile from our home. I felt torn. Stay or go? I worried about evacuating with a young puppy. Martin hadn't been leash-trained yet. Or had travel experience. I took a short drive in the Jeep to see what our neighbors were doing. I noticed their vehicles were loaded and faced out towards the road. Many had trailers hitched up to their vehicles. If we had to go, all of us were ready. Lloyd and I decided to stay. Thankfully, we were never mandated to evacuate.

> "August 12, 2021. Evacuation warnings and orders are in place. Yesterday, up to 1,539 people were evacuated. 1,014 structures remain threatened. Structures remain threatened with Evacuation Orders and Warnings in effect. Road closures are in effect. Hampering containment efforts: Firefighters are working in steep, rugged terrain. A large quantity of standing dead trees and an extremely receptive fuel-bed are made for intense burning within the fire perimeter. Hotspots and smoldering trees continue to be found and extinguished. Long drive to and from incident on long winding roads." (YubaNet)

No kidding about the "long drive." I knew those roads. They were the backroads to our trailer where pavement was nonexistent. Where wells had run dry in June, including ours. I was worried about our neighbors on the hill and called Diane, as she lived slightly northeast of our property.

"Are you safe? Do you need a place to stay?" I asked.

"I tried to drive up the hill yesterday. I got as far as the Ace Hardware parking lot. The road was closed to the north, so I couldn't make it home. I had taken the dogs to the groomers," she said. Diane told me that she had all four dogs with her: her two small terriers and Jerry's two dogs. "I'm staying in Colfax with friends. Jerry and the boys didn't evacuate. They're dragging hoses and ferrying firemen on their ATVs. The roads will be closed for some time, and no one is allowed to enter."

I was relieved to hear Diane had a place to go, and "our boys" were safe.

By August 13, fire behavior was minimal. Firemen felled the hazardous trees and put out hot spots. Multiple dozers had constructed a line around the 184-acre fire. On the 14th, while still under evacuation orders, Diane returned home. It was easy to cross the "road closed" barrier without a human to enforce the order.

"It's crazy up here," she wrote in a text. "There're firemen everywhere." She sent me photos of her scorched driveway and gate, the charred carport next to her trailer.

"Well, it's overwhelming, but my place was saved."

"Did Paul's cabin make it?" I texted back.

"Paul's place is good. I can see it now."

Before the fire, Diane couldn't see Paul's cabin, just a few acres below her trailer. Brush and timber hid it from view. Our trailer was just acres away from Paul's, an easy walk. Later, I would learn that Mike's home had burned down. He was one of our few neighbors who lived on the grid, as his double wide trailer and twenty-acre lot bordered the main road. His eastern property line bordered ours.

On Sunday, the 15th, Lloyd drove out to the trailer. A miracle. No damage. We were filled with relief, yet sad for the folks on the northeast side where a half dozen families had lost their homes. Where would they go? Their homes were off-grid and uninsurable.

By mid-August, many places I had once loved were gone. The Dixie Fire had swelled to over seven hundred thousand acres. The ninety-one-year-old lookout at Mount Harkness in Lassen Park was destroyed. I had camped at nearby Juniper Lake for years and had a friend who lived and worked at the lookout each summer. The town of Greenville was leveled, along with the homes of several longtime friends.

Other fires ravaged Northern California. On August 17th, the Caldor Fire demolished the town of Grizzly Flats in El Dorado County near Lake Tahoe. Grizzly Flats was Lloyd's spirit place. He had hiked and hunted there as a teen. After Lloyd returned from the Vietnam War, he hid from the world in a cabin in Grizzly Flats. It was there, alone in the woods, that he had found solace and healing. He always spoke of returning. When I asked Lloyd how he felt about the loss of Grizzly Flats, he said, "The place is inside me. It will always be there."

Bold sentiments, but I needed landscape, both inside and outside of me. How would I survive without my beloved Sierras? Those mountains that have rooted me. I didn't know, but held on, determined to enjoy each moment with *my* forest.

Closed

As fires surged around us, Jess and Jake received a letter informing them that the FEMA camp they were living in would soon close. I'd often visit Jess and Jake at their trailer, and as summer waned, fewer trailers sat on the FEMA lot. By August, the eighty-eight original trailers had been reduced to five. Where had the families gone? Was there someone, maybe a case worker, who would help them find another home? There wasn't. The FEMA housing was a temporary fix, and time was up. On Tuesday, August 31st, 2021, the FEMA Camp in Chico would close.

Jess and Jake needed a place to stay. The building of their home in Paradise had only recently begun. A foundation was built, but the land lacked water, electricity, and a working septic. I had planned for this interlude by buying a 2018, twenty-five foot, JayCo trailer. It sat on our four-and-a-half-acre lot near our house waiting to be moved to Paradise, but my sons couldn't put the trailer on the Paradise property yet. I discussed the issue with Lloyd.

"Jess and Jake have to move soon, and I had hoped the property in Paradise would be ready for the trailer. It might be another month or so before they can move. Would you be okay if they stayed in the trailer on our property?"

"We can hook up water and electricity, but we can't put the trailer near the septic. They'd have to use the bathroom in the house," Lloyd said. He paused. I felt my heartbeat in my chest; my body tensed. "I don't think that will be a problem. They'll have their own space."

I melted with relief. Lloyd had seen how my sons had lived self-sufficiently in their FEMA trailer keeping it cleaned and maintained. They shopped, cooked, and cared for Jake's daughters each weekend. Lloyd had also seen pictures of the beginnings of the new house in Paradise, so he knew this move had an end point.

On the last day of August, the keys to their FEMA home were returned to a case worker. That night, my sons moved into the trailer on our lot. Jake's drive to work was longer, but doable. Annie and Marie had finally moved into their new house, and with Jake living with Lloyd and me again, the girls would visit our home each weekend. Annie especially loved her time playing with Martin, but neither she nor Marie had forgotten Little Bit.

Each time they visited, they placed a flower or pretty rock on Little Bit's special place.

Marie told me, "I'm sorry about Little Bit. I gave her an apple." I looked over to see one of the yellow apples Marie had found under the apple tree. It was nestled in a cedar plume on top of Little Bit's grave.

Chapter Fifteen
Fall 2021

Layers

In June and August, I had made plans to visit friends in Cedar-ville, the small town where Lloyd and I had escaped to during the fires of 2020. Unfortunately, the fires of 2021 were also ferociously destructive. The one-million-acre Dixie Fire had spread its noxious smoke more than 1,000 miles away, cutting off the backroads towards my destination. I had already canceled my travel plans twice. By mid-October, desperate for some quiet time to write, nap, and chat with my dearest friends, Barbara and Ray, I reserved a room at the only motel in Cedarville. A week later, I packed my Jeep and drove away.

Driving up Historic Highway 49 during high wind warnings, a power blackout, and critical fire conditions, I was struck by the con-trasts in my surroundings. I began my journey toward the high desert under a blue sky and blustery winds. The long green needles of the tall Jeffery and ponderosa pines swayed above the tree-lined road. Brilliant yellow quaking aspen spun and sparkled in the sunlight. The scene was captivating, yet I could not un-remember the fact that much of this tree-dense habitat was unhealthy due to drought. The wind gusts rattling my Jeep placed the forest at high risk for wildfire.

To my right, the North Yuba River gently rolled over boulders, snaked through shallows—water so low that I could see the stones that layered the bottom. Two years earlier, the river rocks were invisible, covered by a foamy whitewater that rushed toward the foothills below.

I continued my drive, dropped into Sierra Valley where gray clouds covered the sun. Strips of darkened fields came into view as a light snow blew horizontally across the road. The tiny, occasional flakes grew thicker. I turned on my windshield wipers, marveled at the wet road and patches of white on the open cattle fields. For almost thirty minutes, I traveled through snow, and then it was gone.

When I reached Highway 395 and headed north, the gales picked up. Dust devils circled my car. The cold increased, but the sky opened. Sunlight streamed through a few lingering clouds. I could see clearly. First, in the town of Doyle, population seven hundred. The devastation from the Beckwourth Complex Fire in July where thirty-three homes were destroyed. Black stumps from burnt sagebrush covered the landscape. Where homes once stood, there were now empty spaces.

Further up the highway in Janesville, where the Dixie Fire had pushed towards the small community, blackened trees stood like skeletons on the hillsides. Most of the structures were saved, but the once-familiar place had become charred and bleak.

The layers of loss since the 2018 Paradise Camp Fire had continued to grow. As forest lands were swallowed up, a hollowness haunted me.

Refuge

Thankfully, my four-day visit in Modoc lifted my spirits. The beauty of the high desert was delicious. The air was biting cold. Smelt like sage and damp grass. It had snowed the night before I arrived, and the jagged peaks of the Warner Mountains were frosted white. The lack of people and vehicles made life slow down. I reveled in the quiet.

Since my last visit in August 2020, the tiny town of Cedarville had lost several businesses on Main Street. The bookstore was gone, along with the local hip coffee shop and a once-popular dinner spot. The old standards still stood: the grocery store and the local restaurant where a hearty ranch breakfast and a decent lunch were served. There were baked goods, too, but dinners were so-so.

As an introvert, I rarely dined out and brought my own breakfast and lunch fixings. Barbara and Ray graciously cooked dinner for me each night. The menus included Ray's delicious buffalo meat loaf, Barbara's shrimp and rice with lime zest, and vegetable pie with puffed pastry crust. They insisted on doing the cooking *and* the dishes, giving me a reprieve from my usual household duties.

Barbara and Ray were generous with their time. Not only did they feed my body, but they also nourished my mind. In the evenings, we shared readings and stories of our life's journeys. They offered me a private writing workshop in a positive and encouraging setting. Curled up on the sofa in front of a toasty fire, popcorn on the coffee table, we shared ideas and insights into each other's written work. One night, Ray gave us a prompt from *The House of Spirits* by Isabel Allende. The line was, "Psst! Father Restrepo! If that story about hell is a lie, we're all fucked aren't we..." The diversity of our short stories created from that simple sentence was pure cognitive fun. Finding friends who shared this passion was rare. Our impromptu workshops restored my inspiration and joy of writing.

The land was still burning, COVID still raged, and an angry stupidity seemed to be the norm for many Americans, yet the acts of kindness shown to me by Barbara and Ray reminded me of the goodness humanity was capable of.

Pumpkins and Rain

Two days after returning home from my visit in the high desert, my family gathered for our annual pumpkin patch ritual. At the rural farm, Annie and Marie picked pumpkins from the leftovers. For many valley farmers, drought, heat, and smoke had reduced their crop size. This included pumpkin farmers. Only a few orange Jack o' Lanterns were left rotting on the ground, so we picked through the small field of mostly white pumpkins.

For Jake, Jess, Karen, my granddaughters, and me, the joy was in the discovery—finding the perfect pumpkin. We liked the ones with knobby skin, the smooth Casper whites, and the green and orange Italian stripes. Our harvest was mostly the smaller Casper's; the only semi-orange pumpkin was an Italian stripe. Marie declared that find a "miracle."

The farm included a play and picnic area, so after our harvest, the girls swung on a rope that hung from the thick branch of a peeling-bark birch. They played on an old-fashioned teeter-totter made from a long plank of metal. There were no grip-handles or safety features. Because Annie outweighed Marie, Annie cautiously tried to find some semblance of balance as Marie grasped the board to keep from falling. Watching this chaotic see-saw scene made my jaws and shoulders tighten. I asked the girls if they might try another activity. When the girls disembarked, we watched in horror as children of different weights sat on each end, the heavier child seated with the board on the ground while the lighter child sat stuck in the air, feet dangling, until the larger child hoped off causing the lighter child to fly into the heavens, then drop to the ground. Annie, always one to rescue someone in need, made several attempts to help the other kids balance on the board.

Back at home, after I had taken a much-needed nap, Annie and I made pumpkin muffins. The warm kitchen smelt like cinnamon. While the muffins baked, Annie and Jess painted their white pumpkins. Jess created a colorful Día de Muertos (Day of the Dead) flowered skull in red, purple, and turquoise. In black paint, Annie drew ghosts, a graveyard and haunted house.

Before evening fell, we walked in the woods with Jackson and Martin. Fallen leaves lay thick on the ground. A golden hue shimmered in the fading sunlight.

That night, it rained. Heavy drops drenched the parched land throughout the evening. I opened my window; the sound of hammering rain hitting the ground soothed me. By the next morning, the deluge had turned to drizzle, but the earth was saturated with wetness, softening my worry of fire. With weather reports of more rains to come, the prospect of ending our hellacious fire season calmed my anxious mind, and I felt something like peace and perhaps pleasure. I put the kettle on the stove, made a cup of coffee, sat in my recliner, and relaxed.

Extremes

In what seemed like minutes, our weather went from extreme fire danger to devastating floods. Whiplash weather. Rain poured down in sheets. Rain so hard I could not motivate my dogs to go outside to pee. No matter how many times I went out the door and stood by myself in the soaking rain, the dogs would not come. I spent an entire day worrying about seven-month-old Martin, afraid he would get a kidney infection from holding his urine so long, but maybe that's just a human trait. By nightfall, both Martin and Jackson took their business outside.

During the night, sleep was hard to come by. The storm was wet, wild, and violent—tree branches crashed to the ground, wind pushed the rain into the windows, hail pelted our metal roof. Still, there was comfort in the rain. Our fire season would soon end. Our scrawny looking plants perked up. The wild white rose bush, the drying raspberries, and the brown grass that once-was-lawn, turned nearly green. Nearby Oroville Lake gained twenty feet of water in one week. There were damages, though. Several roads were closed due to mudslides. Boulders the size of houses had tumbled into the roadways northeast of us. Mud and debris covered highways. Floods filled the lowlands.

When the rains ended, my cupboards were bare, so I drove into town in a world of sunshine, damp-piney-scents, and clarity. On the canyon top—ridge, after ridge of mountains—unfortunately nude due to wildfires—were stunning against the crisp autumn sky. Deep in the canyon where the rivers had been bone-dry, blue waters ran. The trees along the roadside were changing color: orangey-reds, yellows, and golds shimmered in the sunlight. Overwhelmed by the scene, tranquility filled me. Our political world was still chaotic and climate change would continue. Life was a continuous journey through summits and canyons, but those summits sustained me.

When I returned home and pulled into our driveway, our property was filled with tree workers. They were part of the California Forest Stewardship program—created to provide forest landscape restoration and wildfire prevention to extreme fire risk areas. There were about eight workers on our property—some wearing harnesses attached to tree trunks, others clearing and cutting brush. Chainsaws roared, and the ground shook as trees were felled. I liked my forest wild but knew the dead and diseased trees had to come down. The land looked ravaged. It would take weeks to limb, cut, chip, and clear the 200-foot-tall trees, but when the work was completed and the timber neatly stacked, our woods would become healthier—less hazardous.

That evening, I walked along the forest path with the dogs. Scattered bark covered the ground. The jagged-leafed holly shrubs were covered in red berries. Pine needles glowed in the sunny spaces opened by the downed trees. A cacophony of birds sang in the canopy—their music soothing my ever-anxious mind. I could not untangle the links that connected me to this place. They grew stronger as I aged. No matter what our future held, we would rise and fall together.

Epilogue

September 13, 2022. Almost four years since the Paradise Camp Fire destroyed nearly 19,000 homes, businesses, and other buildings. Many people who lived in Paradise before the fire are still without housing, though as of March 2023, Paradise has rebuilt 10,000 homes. Many residential lots are in some form of debris cleanup or rebuilding. Other lots are vacant. If trees remain standing, bare, red dirt covers the landscape, or worse, thick, flammable vegetation. There's a randomness in the placement of homes—a large, new house sits between two vacant lots, or several homes form a row of housing on a mostly-empty street. Many parcels still have temporary housing on the properties—trailers and RVs. Some have connection to water, power, and garbage services. Other families dry camp—meaning they have no connection to such services. Dry campers must rent portable toilets and maintain 500-gallon water tanks. It's difficult for me to drive through Paradise. My heart drops when I take in the scenery. Paradise is scarred. It will take years to heal the landscape, and much of the geography has been changed forever. It's soul crushing.

Jess and Jake had been living in temporary housing from November, 2018 through July 15th of 2022, when their Paradise home finally obtained its certification of occupancy. My sons, their father, and my granddaughters now have permanent places to live. A relative calm has settled into our lives. But summer and autumn in Northern California is still unpredictable as fires rage through communities I know well (Forest Hill and Georgetown are burning due to the Mosquito Fire and The Barnes Fire burns in my beloved Modoc County). And yet. Knowing that my family have houses with water, heat, and air conditioning is a tremendous gift. I am filled with gratitude.

Since Annie and Marie moved into their new home with their mother and stepdad, life has changed for them. Annie isn't as anxious. She has her own room, a special spot for her things—artwork, books, video games. Marie, too, is no longer as agitated. She has a routine, her toys, her own bed. A house isn't just shelter. It's the secure environment where they have the opportunity to thrive.

I want to hold onto this positive ending, but it's difficult after another summer of drought, heat waves, and wild fire. I want the world to care about climate change, to have compassion for our natural environment. I struggle to push down my rising panic. I can't live without the trees. I remember Wendell Berry's poem "Mad Farmer Liberation Front." His words affirm my highest hopes:

> Say that your main crop is the forest
> that you did not plant,
> that you will not live to harvest.
> Say that the leaves are harvested
> when they have rotted into the mold.
> Call that profit.

Author's Note

Much of *Snow After Fire* describes my family's experience in the aftermath of the Paradise Camp Fire. While I do add numbers and information I had learned at the time of my writing, the October 29, 2019, article from *PBS Frontline*, "Camp Fire: By the Numbers" by Priyanka Boghani, provides updated information one year after the fire. For those seeking more knowledge, Frontline's documentary *Fire in Paradise* is highly recommended. Listed below are some of the numbers from the Frontline article.

The fire ignited in the early morning hours of Nov. 8, 2018, and would rage for more than two weeks, devastating the town of Paradise before it was extinguished.

A nearly 100-year-old electrical transmission line owned and operated by Pacific Gas and Electric was identified as the cause of the Camp Fire.

80 football fields a minute was the rate at which the fire spread at its peak.

67 patients admitted at Feather River Hospital were evacuated as the flames approached.

4 hours was all it took for the fire to rip through Paradise.

86 people lost their lives in the fire. Some died in their cars as they were trying to escape.

153,335 acres were burned by the wildfire, approximately the size of Chicago.

18,800 structures were destroyed, most of them — almost 14,000 — were residences.

Around 30,000 people lost their homes.

Throughout my narrative, I mention other fires close to my home: the Berry Creek Fire, the North Complex Fire, the Dixie Fire, the Caldor Fire, and other smaller wildfires, such as the Willow and the Glen Fires in Yuba County, California. When I think of the sheer number of people who have lost their homes in the west due to climate change—I am overwhelmed. Yet, these numbers represent only a tiny fraction of climate-caused devastation to communities throughout the world.

I didn't intend to author a story about fire, housing insecurity, or loss of our wild lands. I simply wrote about my life as it unfolded. Writing was my way to find clarity in an often-confusing world. It provided structure for my messy emotions. It allowed me time to reflect and to discover something to be thankful for during the chaos. It was, and is, how I find hope.

Made in the USA
Monee, IL
03 May 2023